Sound Heal Tuning Forks

Charles Lightwalker

Sound Healing With Tuning Forks

Author: Charles Lightwalker

Copyright © Charles Lightwalker (2023)

The right of Charles Lightwalker to be identified as author of this work has been asserted by the author in accordance with section 77 and 78 of the Copyright, Designs and Patents Act 1988.

First Published in 2024

ISBN 978-1-83538-074-1 (Paperback)

Published by:
    Maple Publishers
    Fairbourne Drive, Atterbury,
    Milton Keynes,
    MK10 9RG, UK

A CIP catalogue record for this title is available from the British Library.

All rights reserved. No part of this book may be reproduced or translated by any form or by any means, electronic or mechanical, including photocopying, recording or by any information storage and retrieval system without written permission from the author.

The views expressed in this work are solely those of the author and do not necessarily reflect the views of the publisher, and the publisher hereby disclaims any responsibility for them.

Table of Contents

Forward	4
Introduction	6
Funing Forks	8
Tuning Forks and Healing	10
How to Use Tuning Forks	14
Using Tuning Forks With The chakra System	18
Other Uses For Tuning Forks	40
Reflex Points	43
Tuning the Organs	47
Body Tuning	53
Aterthoughts	
Articles on Tuning Forks	

Forward to Revised Edition 2023

The time has come to release again this manual/book on sound healing with tuning forks, that I wrote in 2005, and used as a manual with the tuning fork classes I was teaching at that time in my life. I was also working with various other sound healers through the tuning fork research alliance, as we were experiencing the use of tuning forks with other healing modalities and working with research scientists to discover the vibrational frequencies that could be used on specific ailments, illnesses, and problems that were occurring to the human form, and on how to use tuning forks on the treatment of animals. The research is continuing and I have no doubt that the art of healing using tuning forks will expand the health of many and contribute to the knowledge of complimentary care worldwide. May this book contribute to the expanding of knowledge in the sound healing arts.   Charles- summer 2023-Scotland

INTRODUCTION

TUNING FORK PROCESSES
COMMON TERMS USED

- AcuTuning - A process where tuning forks are used to tune the meridian points found in standard acupuncture processes.
- Angel Armour - A process to release stress and tension from the muscle and areas of the body (found in AcuTuning 2 Manual).
- Angel - A Messenger of God or the Divine Presence in all things.
- Chakra - Energy Centers in the body.
- Frequency - The number of repetitions per unit time of a complete wave.
- Grace - This is the life giving energy found in all things.
- Hertz - Measurements of cycles in hundreds.
- HZ - This means hertz.
- Oil - This is referring to the sacred angelic essential oils. These are a blend of essential oils that are blessed and laid to rest to increase their frequencies. For more information see oil information sheet or the Sacred Angelic Oils Manual.
- Prongs - The two ends of the fork, shaped like a U, which vibrate.
- Reflex - The process of pointing the prongs at an area of the body or by placing it on one area of the body to affect another; such as foot reflexology.
- Stem - This is the handle of the tuning fork.
- Tune - Putting an area back into proper frequency. Example: tuning a guitar.
- Tuning Fork Practitioner- a certified tuning fork healer
- TFRA- Tuning Fork Research Alliance

- Tuning Fork Therapist- a term used by some tuning fork practitioners
- Vibration - This is what you feel when the tuning fork is vibrating or moving back and forth.
- Wash - This is where you point the prongs of the tuning fork at the area you are working on.
- Wave - A disturbance or osculation propagated from point to point by mathematical specifications of its amplitude.
- Wave Form - Is the mechanic representation of a wave.

TUNING FORKS

Tuning forks are very precise instruments for producing sounds at a given frequency. They are made out of two basic materials, stainless steel, and aluminum. Aluminum alloy tuning forks are usually used in health and healing applications and emit a tone that is more pure, vibrant, and longer lasting than stainless steel. You are also able to produce overtones and harmonics with aluminum forks that cannot be produced with stainless steel forks. Stainless steel tuning forks are capable of producing only one tone.

The only advantage to stainless steel is that the material is harder than aluminum. Accordingly, more care and gentle handling needs to be given to aluminum tuning forks. It is important to note that regardless of the material being used, all tuning forks are slightly affected by temperature and elevation above sea level. Tuning forks can be purchased with weighted or unweighted ends.

Weighted ends produce a stronger vibration with a louder overall sound that lasts longer and also allows you to better feel the vibration when the stem end is placed on the body. Weighted tuning forks weigh considerably more than standard tuning forks and can be tiring to hold for long periods of time. They also cost considerably more than the standard tuning fork. Unweighted tuning forks are therefore more economical and practical to use for healing purposes.

There are a wide variety of tuning forks available for all types of applications. If there's a frequency, there's a tuning fork ...or two. Tuning forks are all designed around frequencies and the mathematical formulas that determine progressions of frequencies. Some fork sets are based around the mathematics of the solar system, others on the individual planets or their orbits, some on each individual organ of the body as well as individual types of body cells and DNA nucleotides. Tuning forks can be found that supposedly resonate to mineral nutrients, elements, dimensions, the sun, the moon, and a wide range of other non-physical phenomena such as astral projection. Each frequency has a purpose. Do they work? One would have to look for and at results to make this determination or perhaps accept the fact that sometimes things work for reasons that cannot be quantitatively or qualitatively measured. Perhaps it is a matter of faith and intention.

This manual will focus on the use of a standard set of Pythagorean tuning forks and includes several methods for balancing and aligning the Chakras. A variety of tuning forks having special uses will also be presented. Solfeggio Scale tuning forks will also be introduced along with some techniques for their use. Finally, the use of tuning forks in other healing modalities will be presented.

Tuning Forks and Healing

The human body functions harmonically. The frequencies of breathing, blood circulation, the pulse, and all the activities associated with them are intended to function in harmonic balance. Since sound affects us at both the conscious and unconscious levels it has the effect of counterbalancing the physical and emotional states of the body and the mind. By using sound, the internal and external can be brought back into harmony and flexibility. Tuning forks create a resonance throughout our mind, body, emotions, and etheric body. As such, they are powerful tools to facilitate balancing and healing.

A tuning fork, when struck, produces a single sound or note with harmonics and overtones of that note. Strike two tuning forks together and two vibrational frequencies are created. The brain however, hears more than just the two frequencies. It also hears a third frequency derived from the difference between the two forks. So in actuality the brain hears three vibrational frequencies from just the two forks. It follows then, that when multiple forks are used, many harmonics, overtones, and frequencies are experienced. Think of it as bathing in sound.

When tuning forks are used as a tool for healing, the vibrational frequency coupled with the intent can cause a healing effect to occur. The intention for healing to occur must be considered before beginning a session using tuning forks. During a healing session it is not uncommon for others to experience the intention behind the sound. The intention 'rides along' with the sound wave. It is equally important that the client be receptive to the sound and its accompanying intention. This can be accomplished by making sure the recipient is expecting to hear the tones and that he or she is in a relaxed state. It is important to remember that in all aspects of the healing arts the relationship and communication between the practitioner and the client is very important.

A healthy body is in perfect harmonic balance. When the body is out of balance tuning forks can be used to bring about major, positive shifts in the energy patterns within and surrounding the human body. The frequencies generated by the forks act to dissolve negative energy in the aura and chakras. Sound vibration and intent can clear out energy blocks quickly and effectively. During tuning fork therapy, a beneficial process of resonance occurs. As the correct frequency is focused on various parts of the body, new patterns of balance are laid down that essentially can erase old patterns caused by the negative resonance of ill health. If a part of the body is out of balance it will energetically resonate `out of tune'. By applying the correct frequency a resonance is created that entrains the part that is out of balance

back to its correct frequency. The body or body area will only take in and absorb whatever vibrations are needed so sound therapy is a very safe form of therapy to use, even on children. Sound has other effects at conscious and unconscious levels. Sound may often evoke emotional responses and can counterbalance negative emotional states of the body and mind.

Sound can also:

- Energize the body
- Soothe and balance the nervous system
- Lift the spirit
- Promote an almost instantaneous deep state of relaxation
- Promote a meditative state
- Improve mental clarity
- Enhance brain functioning
- Increase mental concentration
- 'Center' the body
- Enhance massage, meditation, Reiki, and acupressure
- Balance and integrate both sides of the brain

- Balance and realign the chakras
- Clear and charge the aura
- Clear and raise the vibrational frequency of a room
- Be used on all acupuncture points and meridians

How To Use Tuning Forks

Tuning forks are very easy to use and take very little practice, without effort or damaging them. It is advisable to practice the various ways to activate tuning forks so that you become comfortable in their use. Remember that these are precision instruments and can be damaged if carelessly used or mistreated.

The tuning fork is generally held one of two ways. The `stem' end is held very gently, a bit loosely, between the fingers at the bottom of the fork. Be sure not to be too close to the body of the tuning fork. If your fingers or hand comes in contact with the vibrating body of the tuning fork the vibrations will stop. The tuning fork can also be placed in the palm of the hand between the thumb and the index finger. When used in contact with the practitioner's palm it is said the vibrations also act as a carrier for channeling the healing energy of the practitioner into the fork, through the fork, and out the fork ends. Be sure not to touch or hang on to the tines of the tuning fork as that will dampen or stop the vibration.

Striking it against a hard rubber object such as a hockey puck, rubber dog bone, or a rubber mallet activates the fork. You can also activate it by striking it against your knee or on the palm of your hand. This will produce a somewhat softer sound. Striking the fork gently on your kneecap can produce a loud sound. You do not need to use a lot of force. A quick flicking motion is all that is required. If a louder sound is desired strike the tuning fork twice in succession against the hard rubber object or gently tap two tuning forks against each other being careful not to nick the edges. If the tuning fork is weighted, the weighted end can be quickly pinched together and released or hit against the heel of the palm of the opposite hand. Do not strike a weighted tuning fork so forcefully that the ends knock together.

It is wise to avoid striking two tuning forks together. If the edges are chipped or dinged the frequency will be altered.

Rarely is this admonition violated but when forks must be struck together it should be done very gently and never on the edges.

If essential oils are used and your tuning forks have painted stems make sure to carefully clean off any oil that might get on them. This will ensure that the paint does not degrade or come off.

Taking care of the tuning forks

The use of Tuning Forks is on the rise within the healing profession. There are a few things to know about tuning forks and their use to have them last you a very long time.

The first is their care. Use a soft rubber object to strike them on. A hockey puck is what we have found to work the best. Also a rubber dog bone works well. Never strike them on anything hard like a table or for that matter hitting them together. This damages the forks and changes their frequencies. And it is the frequencies that are doing the work anyway. Also it is not necessary to hit the fork very hard at all. If you hit it to hard you can bend the fork or damage it and change the frequency. Just lightly tap the fork, usually from the wrist, on the hockey puck. This will cause it to lightly vibrate and you may or may not hear the tone loudly. Some of the forks are very high frequencies and they are not very loud. So louder is not better.

Second is storage. It is best to store them in the bags they came with. This is so they do not clank together or if they do get dropped they have some cushion to fall on. We have a box we carry all of our forks in. You want to make sure that there is a layer of bubble wrap between the layers of forks so that the forks do not clang together in the box as well.

Third is the color on the forks. This can come off. Be careful when using your forks and the oils together. Also if the forks clang together it can result in chipping and peeling of the paint. Avoid striking the handles together to keep the handles the beautiful colors that they are. Due to normal wear and tear on the forks during use the paint may peel. There are a few things that can be done to have the color last longer; wash your hands after handling essential oils and before using the forks, do not bang the forks together, avoid hitting the painted end on anything which can result in chipping, If oil does get on the handle of the forks wipe it off with soap and water, then allow to air dry. Also when using the frequencies for healing, know that no harm can come from applying them to a different area than called for. The frequency will not cause anything to go wrong or cause any damage. It will simply pass through the body unchanged.

Using Tuning Forks with the Chakra System

An assumption is being made that anyone using this manual already possesses an understanding of the Chakra System. A more in-depth presentation on the glands and various states of physical dysfunction associated with each chakra is beyond the scope of this manual. Many fine books are in circulation that contains in-depth presentations of each chakra.

The chakras, the body's energy centers, can be thought of as being a series of steps or lessons one must learn as they ascend from the physical level to the Divine level. Carolyn Myss, in her book "Anatomy of the Spirit", says that each chakra is the center for a particular power. These powers ascend from the densest physical power to the most spiritual power. She states that these powers seem to match the challenges we face in our lives. Each chakra is also associated with various glands and functions of the body.

The standard set of tuning forks can be used in many ways when the characteristics, glands, and powers of each chakra are considered. They may be used to enhance meditation on each chakra, clear out old patterns, release blockages, clear out congestion, physical dysfunctions, and raise our vibratory level to help our efforts to work through or with any of the challenges the chakras represent.

Following are just a few of the many characteristics, issues, emotions, mental areas, and glands in which tuning forks might be of value. The more one knows about the positive and negative attributes or characteristics of the chakra system, the more versatile the tuning forks become.

The Eleven-Chakra System
A Brief Outline by Sherry Fields

The human body contains hundreds of locations where there is focused and concentrated energy. There are, however, twelve major energy centers, commonly referred to as "chakras." Chakra is a Sanskrit word, which means, "wheel." The chakras are similar to wheels in that they are spinning vortexes of energy. They are centers of force located within our etheric body, through which we receive, transmit, and process life energies.

Eastern philosophy has taught a system based on seven chakras for thousands of years and is the basis for spiritual growth in many cultures. Today the angelic realms are teaching a Twelve Chakra system based on lost and forgotten information that will serve as tools to assist humanity in its spiritual journey.

Each chakra in the body is recognized as a focal point for life-force relating to spiritual, physical, emotional, and mental energies. The chakras are the network through which the mind, body, and spirit interact as one holistic system. These major chakras correspond to specific aspects of our consciousness and have their own individual characteristics and functions. Most have a corresponding relationship to one of the various glands of the body's endocrine system, as well as to colors of the rainbow spectrum.

The main purpose in working with and understanding the chakras is to create integration and wholeness within ourselves. In this way we bring the various aspects of our consciousness from the physical to the spiritual, into a harmonious relationship. Ultimately, we begin to recognize that the various aspects of ourselves all work together, and that each aspect is as much a part of the whole as the others. We must be able to acknowledge, integrate, and accept all levels of our being.

To help us in the process of our unfolding it is most important to understand that the chakras are doorways for our consciousness. They are the doorways through which emotional, mental, and spiritual force flow into physical _expression. They are openings through which our attitudes and belief systems enter into and create our mind/ body structure. The energy created from our emotional and mental attitudes runs though the chakras and is distributed to our cells, tissues and organs. Realizing this brings tremendous insight into how we ourselves affect our bodies, minds, and circumstances for better or for worse. To understand the chakras and their relationship to our consciousness is to better understand ourselves. Understanding ourselves will enable us to make our choices and decisions from a place of balance and awareness, rather than being blindly influenced by forces we do not understand.

This outline is a brief description only. For more comprehensive information on the first seven chakras please refer to the many books on the subject. Two good ones are "The Energy of Anatomy" by Carolyn Myss and "The Wheels of Life" by Anodea Judith.

FIRST CHAKRA: ROOT or BASE CHAKRA

Location: Base of the spine (coccyx)
Color: Red (secondary color is black)
Element: Earth
Functions: Gives vitality to the physical body. Life-force survival, self-preservation, instincts survival. Relationship to our tribe, our community, and our family.
Glands /organs: Adrenals, kidneys, spinal column, leg bones.
Gems /minerals: Ruby, garnet, bloodstone, red jasper, black tourmaline, obsidian, and smoky quartz.
Foods: Proteins, Red fruits and vegetables.
Associated aromas: Cedar, Clove
Sensory function: Smell
Qualities /lessons: Matters relating to the material world, success. The physical body, mastery of the body. Grounding, individuality, stability, security, stillness, health, courage, and patience.
Negative qualities: Self-centered, insecurity, violence, greed, and anger.

SECOND CHAKRA: SPLEEN CHAKRA (Sacral Plexus)

Location: Lower abdomen to navel area
Color: Orange
Element: Water
Functions: Procreation, assimilation of food, physical force and vitality, sexuality.
Glands /organs: Ovaries, testicles, prostrate gland, genitals, spleen, womb, and bladder.
Gems /Minerals: Carnelian, coral, gold calcite, amber, citrine, gold topaz, and peach aventurine.
Foods: Liquids: Orange fruits and vegetables.
Associated aromas: Ylang/Ylang, Sandalwood
Sensory function: Taste
Qualities/lessons: Giving & receiving emotions, desire, pleasure, sexual /passionate love, change, movement, assimilation of new ideas. Health, family tolerance, and surrender. Working harmoniously and creatively with others.
Negative qualities: Overindulgence in food or sex, sexual difficulties, confusion, purposelessness, jealousy, envy, desire to possess, emotionalism.

THIRD CHAKRA: SOLAR PLEXUS

Location: Below the breastbone and behind the stomach.
Color: Golden Yellow.
Element: Fire
Functions: It is the center of personal power, ambition, intellect, astral force, desire, and emotions based on intellect and touch.
Glands/organs: Pancreas, liver, digestive tract, stomach, Liver, spleen, gall bladder, autonomic nervous system.
Gems/minerals: Tiger's Eye, Amber, Yellow Topaz, and Citrine.
Foods: Complex Carbohydrates, and Grains.
Associated aromas: Lavender, Rosemary, and Bergamot.
Sensor- function: Sight.
Qualities/lessons: Transforming. Shaping, Purifying, Shaping of Being, Mental Energy.
Negative qualities: Perfectionism, control over self versus others, self-critical thoughts, frustration, anxiety.

FOURTH CHAKRA: HEART CHAKRA

Location: Center of chest, at level of heart.
Color: Green (secondary color is pink).
Element: Air.
Functions: It is the center, which vitalizes the heart, thymus, circulatory system, blood, cellular structure, and involuntary muscles.
Glands/organs: Heart, ribs, chest cavity, lower lungs, and blood, circulatory system, skin, hands, and thymus.
Gems/minerals: Kunzite, emerald, green jade, rose quartz, and pink tourmaline.
Foods: Green vegetables, dark leafy greens.
Associated aromas: Rose oil.
Sensory function: Touch.
Qualities/lessons: The center of compassion, love, group consciousness, and spirituality associated with "oneness" with "all that is." It provides for desegregation between the loving energy of the heart and the analytical energy of the intellect. God connection. Able to give and receive. Open to change and new ideas. Coping with loss. Balance.
Negative qualities: Self-abandonment, fear, sadness, anger, resentment, jealousy, and hostility.

FIFTH CHAKRA: THROAT CHAKRA

Location: Neck, throat area above collarbone.
Color: Blue
Element: The higher _expression of all signs.
Functions: Communication center, acting to provide the energy for, and the understanding of, both verbal and mental communications.
Glands/Organs: Thyroid gland, throat and jaw areas, alimentary canal, lungs, vocal cords, and the breath.
Gems/minerals: Aquamarine, Turquoise, Chalcedony, Chrysocolla.
Foods: Fruit.
Associated aromas: Sage, eucalyptus.
Sensory function: Hearing.
Qualities/lessons: The gateway to the Higher Consciousness and the gateway through which the emotions contained on the heart must pass to become balanced and harmonized. Open, clear communication of feelings and thoughts. Creativity, speaking up, releasing, and healing.
Negative qualities: Uptight, low self-esteem, low self-confidence, hostility, anger, and resentment.

SIXTH CHAKR.A: THIRD EYE (BROW CHAKRA)

Location: Between and about one finger-breadth above the eyebrows.
Color: Indigo
Element: The higher _expression of all signs.
Functions: The center of psychic power, higher intuition, the energies of the spirit, Magnetic forces, and light. Clairvoyance, healing addictions. Central Nervous system.
Gems/minerals: Lapis lazuli, indigo, sapphire, sodalite.
Foods: Chlorophyll, breath, and air.
Associated aromas: Mint, jasmine.
Sensory function: all, inclusive ESP.
Qualities/lessons: Higher consciousness, emotional and spiritual love center, Spiritual inner sight, clairvoyance. When balanced, the mind (right hemisphere) and brain (left hemisphere) function in a Unified field. Insight ensues and its practical application becomes a daily occurrence. It also assists in the purification of negative tendencies and in the elimination of selfish attitudes.
Negative qualities: Worry, hysteria, stress, fear, shock, irritation, depression, headaches, speech and weight problems.

SEVENTH CHAKRA: CROWN CHAKRA

Location: Crown of head.
Color: Violet.
Element: The higher _expression of all elements.
Function: The center of spirituality, enlightenment, dynamic thought and energy. It is the center that vitalizes the cerebrum, the right eye, and the pineal gland.
Glands/organs: Pineal gland, cerebrum.
Gems/minerals: Amethyst, quartz crystal.
Foods: Sun, juice, fasting.
Associated aromas: Galbanum, lotus.
Sensory function: None
Qualities/lessons: It allows for the inward flow of wisdom from the ethers and brings the gift of cosmic consciousness. When stimulated and clear, it enables one to see the truth concerning illusory ideals, materialistic pursuits, self-limiting concepts, pride, and vanity; it further allows one to experience continuous self-awareness and conscious detachment from personal emotions, compassion, seeing self in others, peacefulness, oneness.
Negative qualities: Confusion, anxiety, stress.
Additional Chakras as described by Metatron

EIGHTH CHAKRA - INFRA RED – OMEGA

Location: Midway between the root chakra and the knees
Color: Infrared, a combination of red and blue
Function: An energy transference chakra. It takes in energy from the world and other people, plants and animals and operates like a step-down or step-up transformer. Seeing the whole body and the Chakras as an integrated energy system, the Omega transfers energy from outside the body to inside increasing or decreasing it as necessary to stimulate energy flow and release blocks.
Qualities/lessons: It is also like a two-way valve, we can use the Omega to release stored/stagnant Chi or energy, or for clearing a block/learning the lesson. Used to release also when we ask the angels/spirit to assist us to transmute negative thoughts and belief systems, past words, actions or deeds.
Negative qualities: Inactivity/sloth, emotionalism - empathic abilities run riot, getting into other people's stuff and not focusing on self growth.

NINTH CHAKRA - ULTRA VIOLET – ALPHA

Location: Between 12 and 18 inches out from the top of the head.
Color: Ultra Violet - blue and violet
Function: This chakra is the access to information about Karma, lessons, our learning abilities, doorways to dimensions and times as well as the Akashic records. When we access past life information it is through this chakra. Occasionally we can access this information in the dream state, when there is important information to be communicated to us. Often spirit/angels will use this tool to get our attention. The dream state many times expresses ideas in symbols and it is our job to interpret the symbols presented. We can of course gain confirmation of our interpretation through meditation. But first the idea or lesson must be accessed.
Qualities/lessons: Innate knowledge of the law of Karma, other dimensions and Akashic records, past life interpretation
Negative qualities: Too much reliance on outside guidance, looses communication with the higher self within.

TENTH CHAKRA - SILVER – TERRA

Location: Midway between the knees and the feet.
Color: Silver
Function: The Grounding Chakra, a receptive energy with a positive flow containing the elements of wind, earth, water and fire. It is the anchor to the physical world. We are spiritual beings having a physical experience. We need to stay balanced, emotionally, mentally, physically and spiritually.
Equally the chakras must be balanced. We are not just to work on the spiritual or upper chakras, but all of them equally. We are here in the physical for a purpose to learn and grow through the experience. It is through the Terra Chakra that we ground and connect to the earth (Gaia). This is where our sense of knowing 'nature' develops and understanding the naturalness of the cycles of life. Birth, growth then death. It is repeated everywhere in nature, in the plant life, the animal life, the mineral life even in the cosmos.
Qualities/lessons: Keeping balance here helps us to stay grounded and understand the nature of our life, the cycles and the patterns within it. It allows us to develop our natural knowing.
Negative qualities: In the unbalanced, ungrounded state we develop fears about the cycles of life, loose connection with our spiritual knowing.

ELEVENTH CHAKRA - GOLD – ANGELIC

Location: Between 18 and 24 inches out from the top of our head
Color: Gold
Function: The angelic chakra contains the programming of the soul for this lifetime and the history of the soul. It is through our connection and understanding of this chakra that we gain or

affect our own healings, insights, learn our lessons, understand the soul contracts and begin to understand our life purpose.

Qualities/lessons: As we continue to evolve as physical/spiritual beings our understanding of this chakra is strengthened. We can begin to see (re-remember) the goals we came into this life to achieve. As we grow in understanding we can endeavor to achieve those goals by living our life in the flow of its purpose instead of against it.

Negative Qualities: None, communication from the angelic realm cannot be negative.

Chakra Balancing

Tuning forks are an effective and fast way to balance the Chakra system. The Chakras can be balanced using a standard set of seven or eight Pythagorean tuning forks, or a set of seven Solfeggio tuning forks. Instructions will also be given for using a set of seven tuning forks to balance a system of twelve chakras.

For the procedures to follow we will use a standard set of seven Pythagorean tuning forks. These forks span a tonal range from C at 256 Hz to B at 481 Hz. Some sets will include an eighth fork, which makes a full octave of sound, but this isn't required for balancing the seven chakras.

If a chakra is out of balance in any way, closed down, too small, not circular in spin, or out to the side, exposure to the tones will cause it to immediately realign, balance, and open up. It may take several balancing sessions to `train' an out of balance chakra to hold or remain in a balanced position. In a sense, the chakra must `forget' the frequency of being out of balance and `learn' the new and correct frequency. Of course any personal or health issues that might be the source of imbalance must be addressed.

To begin all procedures the tuning forks will be activated as described earlier and either held over the chakra, circled over the chakra, or have the stem end placed on the chakra. Let your intuition guide you as to what is required. Several methods of chakra balancing will be presented.

Balancing and Opening the Chakras

This method balances all seven of the chakras. Start with the C and G tuning forks to relax the client. This is the Body Tuning process presented earlier in the manual.

If you have the Shekinah and Michael tuning forks from Angel Gate Creations you can use the Shekinah tuning fork to ground the client and the Michael fork to call in Spirit. Additional information on these tuning forks is located in the section titled Angel Forks.

Tone the C tuning fork and begin to balance the system starting at the root chakra and proceed up through the 7th or Crown chakra.

Once activated keep the tuning fork several inches above the chakra, about 6 to 8 inches will do. It is not necessary to be any closer. Point the ends of the tuning fork down and over the chakra. You may also move the tuning fork around the chakra in a clockwise motion to vibrationally encourage the chakra to open further. Hold the tuning fork in this position for approximately 20 to 30 seconds or until you can no longer hear or feel the vibration.

If your set has an eighth tuning fork you may use it for the Transpersonal chakra. You may then also use the C and G forks again, or the Creation fork, to sweep the body from head to toe or circle the body to balance and seal the etheric fields.

When using the tuning forks to balance your own chakras you might try visualizing the colors of each chakra as you tune them. Visualize a ball of color at the location of the chakra and as you hear the sound, draw it into the ball of color.

Chakra Connecting

This method of balancing the chakras can be done using the techniques of presented in Chakra Balancing.

As they are tuned and balanced each chakra will be linked with the one directly above it. Start at the root chakra and balance it. Before you finish with this chakra slowly sweep the energy up to the sacral chakra, thus making an energy link from the root chakra to the sacral. Now, proceed on to tune the sacral chakra and finish with a sweep up to the solar plexus. Balance the remaining chakras in this manner. As you finish with the crown chakra sweep the energy around the body's auric field from top to bottom three times.

Balancing the Chakras with a Heart Link

This method will involve keeping a link between the heart and each of the seven chakras as they are balanced. Use any of the Chakra Balancing techniques. The practitioner will hold their right hand over or lightly touching the heart chakra while balancing each chakra with the tuning forks held in the left hand. The frequency of the tuning forks will also travel directly to the chakras through the body of the practitioner, through the heart, and out of their right hand down to the heart of the client. The healing energy the practitioner brings to the session will also pass to the client along with the tuning fork vibrations. At the heart chakra hold the tuning fork over the hand that is holding position over or on the heart.

To avoid having crossed arms it will be necessary to switch sides of the table to complete the remaining chakras from the Throat to the Crown.

Balancing the Chakras to the Heart

This variation of chakra balancing will balance the lower chakras as in Chakra Linking except that all chakras will balance to the Heart and not beyond. The lower chakras will balance up to the Heart and the upper chakras will balance down to the Heart.

Balance the Root chakra and sweep the vibration up to the Heart. Next balance the Sacral chakra and sweep the vibration up to the Heart as well. Repeat with the Solar Plexus chakra. The upper chakras will balance and sweep down to the Heart chakra in the same manner the lower chakras were balanced. The Heart chakra will be balanced last.

One way to complete this session is to hold all of the tuning forks except the Heart tuning fork in the left hand and very gently activate them by striking them with the Heart fork in order from Root to Crown. Be very careful not to strike the tuning forks too hard or the tines may get dinged or chipped. Do not strike the tuning forks directly on their edges. Wash over the entire body with the tuning forks, starting at the feet and coming back to end at the Heart chakra. The sound of all the tuning forks activated at once is very harmonious and soothing to the client.

Chakra Readings

All sorts of energies and issues may be found in the chakras. The chakras are funnel shaped and have four wheels or rings within them that correspond to the physical, emotional, mental and spiritual bodies. The innermost rings in this spiraling energy are smaller than the outside rings. Healthy rings spin clockwise in the northern hemisphere (opposite in the southern hemisphere). The chakras in front of the person represent the conscious and the chakras in back of the person represent the unconscious. There is a chakra bridge in between. Always read and assist in clearing the front chakras first.

If any chakras are spinning counter clockwise (in NH), start the clearing there. Some reasons for a counter clockwise spin are:
1. A physical whack
2. A very intrusive cord
3. Clingy control energy
4. Lots of foreign energy with a charge on it.
5. Chakra is releasing something.

You can use a pendulum to ask which direction a chakra is rotating. With practice you can tell by feeling with your hand or just trust your knowing.

Reading and Clearing the Chakras:

1. Put a picture of the chakra on your screen. Throw purple at it and see if it sticks anywhere. Run your hand over the screen to feel for cords and foreign energy. Listen for guidance, pay attention to the first thought that enters your mind. Look at the front first and then the back.
2. Look for pain, perfect pictures, whacks, other people, belief systems, thought forms, cords, and contracts.
3. Ask the person's higher self what is appropriate to assist in clearing at this time. Person may not be ready to let go of some things as they are still serving them in some way.
4. Decording - Do not take out cords the person may still be dependent on or good cords (i.e. between the heart chakras of lovers, between mothers and young children). There may be homework for the person to do if there is a dependent cord. The person may go into shock or terror if it is removed prematurely. If the cord is to be removed, take it out with a rose. If it won't stay out, there is probably a contract that needs to be cleared attached to the cord.

5. To clear contracts have the client mentally write it on a piece of paper, rip it up and violet flame it. To clear beliefs and perfect pictures, have the client visualize a snap shot of the belief, stamp cancel all over it and violet flame it.
6. Erase pain, reweave whacks with golden filaments.
7. Other people - ask why person has let someone else into their chakra; there may be a contract or belief. Once reason is cleared, have client push a picture of the person outside of their aura with their breath and blow them up in a rose.

Preparing to Do a Reading

1. Put down a grounding cord. Pull your aura into 18 to 24 inches from your body.
2. Contact and acknowledge your higher self. Ask for assistance with the reading and healing.
3. Put fresh roses around your aura.
4. Adjust your first, second and third chakras.
a. Adjust the first and second chakras to ten percent open. This helps you to be in a healthy state of detachment and not take on other people's emotions. It allows your clairsentience to be more open and feel the energies.
b. Adjust your third chakra to 70 percent open for women and 50 percent open for men. This allows you to have more confidence in yourself and the information you are receiving.
5. Place a large neutralizing Reading and Healing Rose with a grounding cord between your aura and the client's aura with the intent that it will take on cords, energies etc. that are clearing from the other instead of getting into your space.
6. Place a Matching Picture Rose between your and their auras. When you have a matching issue it will pull energy out of the energy field, acting like a photocopier, healing you as well.
   a. Optional - Place a matching picture rose at each chakra.
7. Observe the color of their Crown Loop on your screen and match yours one shade (frequency) lighter. You may set your crown loop color by intention. This keeps you from drawing their energy into your aura.
8. Put up your "TV" reading screen between your aura and the reading and healing rose. Option- connect two grounding cords to the screen.
9. If someone is blocking the screen or trying to get into your space, hook them up to the Supreme Being and have them pulled out of your space.

10. Visualize a golden sun above your head and bring the light down through your crown chakra through the pineal gland, to the throat, then down both arms ending in the palms of your hands. Run the energy across the screen to clear it.

11. Ask the client to say their name three times and touch the screen to feel it as they are saying it. This will give you a sense of their energy signature.

a. If their current name is not the same as their birth name, have them say their birth name twice and their current name twice.

b. Option: ground them on the screen.

12. Anchor your crown loop to the four corners of the room. This helps you own the space during the reading.

13. Tune into their being, in and out of their body. Say hello to their Higher Self and ask permission to do the reading. (Sometimes they say no.)

Ending a Reading
Making Separations:

1. Blow the matching picture rose.
2. Put the client's face in a rose and run it through your aura to pick up any energy that may have stuck to you.
3. Blow the healing rose.
4. Visualize a golden ring with a piece missing and ask that anything that has not been completed in the reading be completed. Fill in the missing space with golden light. Then blow the ring up in a rose.
5. Tear and burn the contract between you and the other person. "My agreement to do this reading is now complete in the physical and other realms /realities".
6. Do five physical separations. Look at the person and identify five things about them that is not you. That is them, it is not me.
7. Affirm "My energy will run in perfect order to take care of me. My energy will run in a way that is in affinity with me."
8. Allow the chakras to come back to normal operating percentages. Put any second chakra stuff in a second chakra rose and blow it up.

OTHER USES FOR TUNING FORKS

Once activated the tuning fork can be used in several different ways depending on the type of treatment being given or its intended use. To determine which tuning fork to use, consider the intention behind the action. To raise the vibratory level before a healing session, a class, or meditation, choose a fork with a high frequency, such as the tuning fork that vibrates to the note of B. If the intention is to ground an individual or a room, use a tuning fork of a lower frequency such as the tuning fork for the note C. The Solfeggio tuning forks are an excellent choice for use in healing when intention is being considered but the Pythagorean tuning forks are equally useful.

Here are some other ways to use tuning forks:

1. The tines (ends) can be pointed at the area to be treated allowing the vibration to focus onto or into the specific part of the body, organ, energy block, or area of discomfort or pain.
2. Sound energy from the ends of the tuning fork can be focused directly into the center of a chakra or meridian point. Keep several inches between the fork and the client.
3. The energy can be spiraled into and around a chakra to balance and gently open the chakra even further.
4. The tuning fork can be `washed' over a large area, bathing the area in vibration. To enhance spiritual states try using one or more of the tuning forks that have a high frequency. Useful in enhancing your personal space.
5. The fork can be waved around the body to clear, charge, balance, or clean the auric field. You would use a tuning fork with a high vibration.

6. Activate more than one fork and stroke the chakras, the body's energy field, meridian lines, or the entire body.
7. Use two tuning forks, such as the C and G fork, to balance the body, left / right, front / back or top / bottom.
8. The stem end can be placed directly onto an area to send the vibrations into the tissues, bones, joints, muscles, energy block, acupuncture points, acupressure points, energy tines, chakras, etc.
9. Tuning forks can be used with crystals. One example would be to direct a crystal point, one whose other end is flat, towards a chakra, activate a tuning fork and touch the stem end of the tuning fork to the flat end of the crystal. The tuning fork vibration will be enhanced as it passes through the crystal. If you use crystals or stones in your chakra or Reiki sessions you can charge them using the tuning fork that corresponds to the chakra. Activate the tuning fork, point it, move it around, or touch the stem end to the crystal or stone.
10. Use the stem end to charge objects such as, crystals, stones, water, etc. Activate the tuning fork and place the stem end gently against the object. Water can be charged by actually gently touching the surface of the water with the tines of an activated tuning fork two or three times.
11. Charge your food by sweeping over it with a tuning fork. Perhaps a good choice would be a tuning fork that has an attribute or characteristic of gratitude or love. The tuning fork for the heart chakra, the note F, would be a good choice.
12. Tuning forks can be used to set the vibrational level of a room prior to or after an event. Use a high vibration tuning fork to bring in Spirit. Use a low vibration tuning fork to ground the room.
13. Tuning forks can be used in a wide variety of other healing uses such as Reiki, hypnotherapy, massage, reflexology, yoga, meditation, color therapy, psychotherapy, pain management, and sports rehabilitation.

14. In any healing application, for example Reiki, tuning forks can be used to set the vibrational level of the room, ground the client, call in higher vibrations, and tune the client for the session (see Body Tuning and Om fork). The Reiki symbols can also be drawn in the air using a tuning fork such as the Om, Creation, or any of a high vibration.
15. You can learn to use your voice to resonate with the sound of a tuning fork. Hum with the sound of the tuning fork and later use your mind to produce the sound. By practicing this you can then carry the sound of the frequencies internally and resonate with any fork at any time. The Om fork might be a good tuning fork to learn to hum to. This process is called Toning and was developed by John Beaulieu, N. D. founder of The BioSonic Academy.

Remember, the more you use and experiment with tuning forks the more uses you will discover for them. It is helpful to keep a log of how you use your tuning forks along with a notation of the effect or results from each use. Keep in mind that not all clients will respond in the same way to the use of tuning forks.

Reflex Points

In this section you are given two aspects to consider in sound or vibrational therapy. First, are the symptoms that occur in the body and secondly, reflexing the areas on the body to take care of the problems. You will be using tuning forks, which produce the proper sound in Hz to assist the body in healing. Lets say for the sake of argument that every part of our body resonates at a different frequency. A healthy body is in tune. The body is like a huge orchestra that is playing the grand symphony of your life. When everyone is in tune and playing at the same beat it works. If someone is having a bad day, or is thinking about something negative, or maybe playing out of tune, it doesn't work.

Every organ of our body has a frequency or a note playing at the same time. This creates harmonics that give us health. If the frequency is too low, a string is too loose. If the frequency is too high, it is to tight. Or the string can snap. No matter what it is you hear it is still out. With the body you can't hear what is out, however the body will produce SYMPTOMS to let you know something is out. In its own way it is telling you it needs to be tuned. The symptoms do not necessarily mean that's where or what the problem is. The whole body and everything in it are connected. If something is out somewhere a symptom may show up somewhere else. Which may be the place we should be working on rather then trying to take care of the symptom. How we do this is to reflex the place where the problem is. This means there is a place on the body to send a frequency to correct what is out. This brings it back into tune, like tapping your knee and your leg moves. You have reflexed the knee with a force and produced an action. The same holds true with tuning forks when reflexed to a point on the body. It will in turn cause an action on the rest of the body. To reflex the area or wash over it, simply point the prongs of the fork (after it is vibrating) at the area you are reflexing to. Listed below are symptoms that show up and where to reflex the sound; in other words, where to point the tuning fork.

C or Red Fork *Symptom:* poor circulation, iron deficiency anemia and blood disorders, paralysis, swollen ankles and cold feet, lumbago, stiff joints, constipation or diarrhea, sadness.
Reflex to: colon, neck, knees, nose

D or Orange Fork *Symptom:* asthma, bronchitis, gout, gallstones, obesity, purification and removal of toxins and poisons, lethargy and apathy
Reflex to: breasts, reproductive organs, perinea floor, feet and tongue
E or Yellow Fork *Symptom:* constipation, indigestion, flatulence, liver and gastrointestinal disorders, coughs, headache, poor skin condition, sluggishness, boredom

Reflex to: head, eyes, solar plexus, umbilical area, and thighs
F or Green Fork *Symptom:* hay fever, allergies, head colds, trauma and shock, colic, exhaustion, ulcers, sleeplessness, high blood pressure, irritability, back pain, dry skin
Reflex to: kidneys, shoulder, chest colon, suprarenal gland, calves, and ankles

G or Blue Fork *Symptom:* Laryngitis, tonsillitis and throat infections, headaches, eye problems, skin disorders and itching, vomiting, muscular spasms, menstruation pains, fevers
Reflex to: reproductive system, saliva, and hair

A or Purple Fork *Symptom:* nervous ailments, convulsions, obsessions, balance disorders, excessive bleeding, swelling and palsy, shingles
Reflex to: sacrum (base of spine)

B or Violet Fork *Symptom:* neuralgia, cramps and inflammatory pains, glandular imbalance, immune deficiency, processing vitamins, goiters, and nervous disorders
Reflex to: entire body

TUNING THE ORGANS

The Organ Tuning Forks

Just like a symphony orchestra, when the organs are all in balance and healthy they sing a harmonic song of wholeness. But when one or more organ is out of balance or diseased they create a dis-functoning system effecting the other organs. By using the Organ Tuning Fork Set one can retune the organs back into balance creating a synergistic healthy flow of life force energy. This chapter explains the process and procedure necessary to retune or rebalance the organs into a normal healthy function.

The set has 14 forks, one for each of the major organs and essential parts of the physical body. These forks are tuned to the frequencies of healthy human tissue. They can be used to elevate the body to a balanced state of health. They most efficient used in conjunction with the chakra forks in healing, but can also be used individually for a specific issue. To bring the body into alignment, balance the charkas first & then use the Organ Tuning Fork Set to correct the frequency of each organ.

The human body uses its organs to support it in staying balanced. For example if the lungs are not operating at the level of efficiency that they were meant to be, the oxygen to the rest of the body is lessened. From this the rest of the body does not have what it needs to operate correctly. When we can change the way an organ is functioning, we can get the body back into balance.

To assist you in retuning the organs find listed the organs and the fork(s) to use in the process. Tap the tuning fork to get it vibrating and place the stem on or over the organ until it stops vibrating. This will assist in releasing stagnant energy, which isn't serving the organ well. Then to put energy into the organ turn the fork the other way around so that the stem is facing away from the organ.

Another way to retune the organs is by applying the tuning forks to the reflex points on the bottom of the feet. This is great if there are some difficult areas to reach. The client doesn't need to undress for the processes - you can just have him/her remove shoes and socks.

The Organs Tuning Fork Set is considered an advance set, and can be used to balance certain organs or to clear a specific emotions or issues. Using a specific Organ tuning fork to clear a specific emotion or issue can be more direct and save time when used with other healing modalities. Find below a list of the organs & their corresponding note, frequency and relevant emotions or thoughts, which could create imbalance.

Blood - E 321.9 Hz. Lack of Joy.
Adrenals - B 492.8 Hz. Anxiety.
Kidneys - Eb 319.88 Hz. Fear, disappointment, failure.
Liver - Eb 317.83 Hz. Anger.
Bladder - F 352 Hz. Anxiety, fear of letting go.
Intestines - C# 281 Hz. Assimilation & absorption.
Lungs - A 220 Hz. Grief, depression, unworthy.
Colon - F 176 Hz. Releasing the past.
Gall Bladder - E 164.3 Hz. Pride, hard thoughts.
Pancreas - C# 117.3 Hz. Deep sorrow, a need to control.
Stomach - A 110 Hz. Fear of the new, dread.
Brain - Eb 315.8 Hz. Stubborn, fear, self criticism, refusing to change.
Muscles - E 324 Hz. Resistance to new experiences.

Adrenals Tuning Fork

This fork is to bring balance to the adrenals, and is tuned to the frequencies of a healthy adrenal gland. It can be used to elevate the adrenals to a balanced state of health. Strike the fork on a rubber hockey puck to get it vibrating then wave the fork over the area of the adrenals for 20 seconds. Repeat the process again for another 20 seconds.

Bladder Tuning Fork

This fork is to bring balance to the Bladder, and is tuned to the frequencies of a healthy Bladder. It can be used to elevate the bladder to a balanced state of health. Strike the fork on a rubber hockey puck, then wave the tuning fork over the Bladder area, this will bring the Bladder into balance.

Blood Tuning Fork

This fork is to bring balance to the blood system, and is tuned to the frequencies of a healthy blood system. It can be used to elevate the blood to a balanced state of health. Strike the fork on a rubber hockey puck, then while vibrating place the fork 8 inches above the heart area, waving the fork for 20 seconds. This will send the vibrational frequency into the blood stream creating a healthy flow of blood.

Brain Tuning Fork

The brain takes on external stimuli through the sensory system. Touch, taste, smell, sight and sound are all transmitted to the brain, however the connections that allow brain cells to process this information will become distorted if lacking the proper stimulation. Sensory deprivation has a significant impact on the brain.

Balancing the Sides of the Brain

Stand at the head of the healing table facing the person lying on the table face up. Tap the Brain fork to start it vibrating, then place the fork with the stem placed on the right side of the temple for 20 seconds. Then repeat the process on the left temple, for 20 seconds. Tap the fork again and move the fork to above the ears (in the small indentation), tap the fork again and do the other side (above the ear) for 20 seconds. Tap again and place the stem in the small indentation behind the ear lobe. Repeat to other ear. Next tap again and place the stem of the brain fork on the crown of the head. Then use the Om fork by placing the Om fork (when vibrating) 4 inches from the ear for 20 seconds, the repeat the process on the other ear. This will bring the brain organ back into a balanced frequency.

Colon Tuning Fork
This fork is to bring balance to the colon, and is tuned to the frequencies of healthy colon. It can be used to elevate the organ to a balanced state of health. Strike the fork on a rubber hockey puck, once the fork is vibrating wave the fork over the colon area for 20 seconds, this will bring the colon into harmonic balance.

Gall Bladder Tuning Fork
This fork is to bring balance to the Gall Bladder, and is tuned to the frequencies of a healthy Gall Bladder. It can be used to elevate the Gall Bladder to a balanced state of health. Strike the fork on a rubber hockey puck, once the fork is vibrating wave the fork over the Gall Bladder area for 20 seconds, this will bring the Gall Bladder into harmonic balance.

Intestines Tuning Fork
This fork is part of the Organ Tuning Forks Set. This fork is to bring balance to the Intestines, and is tuned to the frequencies of healthy Intestines. It can be used to elevate the Intestines to a balanced state of health. Strike the fork on a rubber hockey puck, once the fork is vibrating wave the fork over the Gall Bladder area for 20 seconds, this will bring the Gall Bladder into harmonic balance.

Kidneys Tuning Fork

This fork is to bring balance to the kidneys, and is tuned to the frequencies of healthy kidneys. It can be used to elevate the kidneys to a balanced state of health. Strike the tuning fork on a rubber hockey puck, once the tuning fork is vibrating wave the tuning fork over the Kidney area, this will bring the Kidney into balance.

Liver Tuning Fork
This fork is to bring balance to the liver, and is tuned to the frequencies of healthy liver tissue. It can be used to elevate the liver to a balanced state of health. Use the Liver tuning fork by striking the fork on a rubber hockey puck, once the tuning fork is vibrating, wave the tuning fork over the Liver area, this will bring the Liver into balance.

Lungs Tuning Fork
This fork is to bring balance to the Lungs, and is tuned to the frequencies of healthy Lungs. It can be used to elevate the Lungs to a balanced state of health. Use the Lung tuning forks by striking it on a rubber hockey puck, once the fork is vibrating wave the fork over the lungs over 20 seconds, this will bring the Lungs into balance.

Muscles Tuning Fork
This fork is to bring balance to the Muscles, and is tuned to the frequencies of healthy Muscles. It can be used to elevate the Muscles to a balanced state of health. Use the Muscles tuning fork by striking it on a rubber hockey puck, once the fork is vibrating wave the fork over the Muscles of the body (especially over muscles that are sore, strained or injured), this would bring the Muscles into balance.

Pancreas Tuning Fork
This fork is to bring balance to the Pancreas, and is tuned to the frequencies of a healthy Pancreas. It can be used to elevate the Pancreas to a balanced state of health.

Stomach Tuning Fork

This fork is to bring balance to the stomach, and is tuned to the frequencies of healthy stomach tissue. It can be used to elevate the stomach to a balanced state of health. Use the Stomach tuning fork by striking it on a rubber hockey puck, once the fork is vibrating wave the fork over the stomach area for 20 seconds, this will bring the Stomach into balance.

Body Tuning

Body Tuning is a phrase coined by John Beaulieu, N.D., author of "Music and Sound in the Healing Arts", that describes the use of tuning forks called Body Tuners. Body Tuning is a powerful way of using sound vibrations to resonate the body, brain, and etheric fields. The specific tuning forks used are a C fork of 256 Hz and a G fork of 384 Hz.

These two forks vibrate at a ratio of 2:3, which is considered sacred in many traditions that have an understanding of the relationship of mathematics to the universe. These two forks, when used in combination, produce a perfect fifth interval and are said to open a gateway for healing and higher consciousness. John Beaulieu, N.D., says that this fifth interval has many benefits such as counteracting depression, making joints more mobile, balancing the earth with the spirit, balancing the heart, pituitary gland, and sphenoid bone as well as balancing the sympathetic and parasympathetic nervous system.

When both forks are struck and brought to the ears the brain hears a third tone that brings the entire nervous system into balance and integrates the mind and body. Within 30 seconds it may be possible to reach a state of deep relaxation that might otherwise take you 45 minutes to achieve through meditation alone. They also balance both hemispheres of the brain, the auric field, and release energy blocks. The tones can alleviate depression, improve joint mobility, and balance the spirit with the earth. This method can also be used to prepare a client for any type of healing session including chakra balancing.

Procedure

Strike both forks and bring them to your ears or the ears of your client. You may strike the forks as often as is necessary to let them experience the tones and create a deep resonance within the head. Make sure to switch sides with the forks as you do this. You might also use the forks to wash over the body or sweep the energy field. Let your intuition guide you in this regard.

USING TUNING FORKS WITH REFLEXOLOGY

Tuning forks can also be use when giving a reflexology treatment. Using any reflexology chart you need only locate the desired reflexology point. Then, using a chakra chart that lists the body organs associated with each individual chakra, find the chakra that corresponds to the desired organ or body part.

From this it is easy to choose the appropriate tuning fork to be used. For example, if the reflexologist needed to work on the reflex point related to the spleen, they would use a chakra chart and note that the spleen was related to the Sacral chakra. The Sacral chakra corresponds to the "D" tuning fork. So the reflexologist would use the "D" tuning fork to work on the spleen reflex point. The tuning fork would be used by activating and placing the stem directly on the reflex point or allowing the vibrations to wash over the area.

In the case of reflexing a kidney point the reflexologist would choose two tuning forks, the "C" and the "D", since the kidneys are related to both the Root and the Sacral chakra. They could be used individually, one at a time, or together by striking them together carefully.

A List of Tuning Forks

The Ozone (O₃) Fork

03 is the symbol for ozone, three oxygen molecules bonded together. Ozone in the atmosphere keeps our planet and the life on it safe from the harmful effects of ultraviolet radiation. Ozone has other useful properties such as keeping the air inside our homes clean. Ozone purifiers remove harmful bacteria, viruses, dust, and other allergens from the air.

Ozone is an unstable molecule. To become stable it must lose one of its oxygen molecules and become 02. The molecule thrown off attaches to viruses or bacteria and kills them. It also attaches to dust and allergens and removes them from the air we breathe.

Ozone has yet another very important benefit to humans. When abnormal cells are subjected to ozone they cannot reproduce more of themselves. When the abnormal cell, such as a cancer cell, is prevented from reproducing, our immune systems can then attack and destroy them.

Ozone can be produced by a thunderstorm, by man made devices, or by the human body. The ozone fork vibrates at a bit over 78 Hz, which is above the range needed to produce ozone in the body. The frequency of ozone in the body and the frequency of the tuning fork will resonate at the same frequency. This will enhance the production of ozone in the body wherever the fork is placed. The ozone fork can be washed over the body area or placed directly on the spot that needs treatment.

To Use

If an infection or virus is present point the tines at the infection and wash over the area as needed. You may also place the stem on any spot where there might be a virus problem allowing the vibration to enter the body.

For tumors, place the stem on the tumor. The vibrations will prohibit the growth of abnormal cells allowing the immune system to take over and destroy them. Keep in mind that with any medical problems you still need the advice and treatment of medical professionals.

The ozone fork is also used on any of the points that are used for viral or bacterial treatments in Acupuncture, Acupressure, or AcuTuning. It is available from Angel Gate Creations, www.teachonlylove.com.

The Nerve Fork

A nerve fires at a frequency of 50 Hz carrying a message from the brain or to the brain. When some trauma to the body occurs, the nerve tells the brain something is out. The brain reacts to this process by correcting it. If the damage is too great for the brain to repair easily, it starts sending endorphins to ease the pain. If the damage is to the nerve, the frequency for information is hindered in the flow to the brain.

This tuning fork can be used to relive pain from pulled or strained muscles. It is also excellent fork for removing those knots that develop in the muscles. It will help in releasing the tightness of cramps so that the muscle will relax and the brain will send the endorphins to help with the pain. Place the end of the stem on the area where there is pain. You may also place the side of the stem in the same area. On the weighted end of the tuning fork pinch the two ends together and slide your fingers off quickly. Hitting the end of the fork on a hard rubber object is not needed to cause the maximum amount of vibration.

For wounds and bruises DO NOT place the stem side of the tuning fork on the area. Instead pinch the end of the tuning fork and point that at the wound or bruise moving in a circular motion.

Knots in the Muscle

Place the stem point of the Nerve fork on the knot in the muscle. Pinch the end of the fork to make it vibrate. If this causes pain you may want to vibrate the fork and then roll the side of the stem over the spot first to loosen it up. REMEMBER you don't have to press hard to have the vibrations work on the muscle. Once you have sent the 50 Hz into the muscle you will want to place Michaels oil over the spot. Again use the 50 Hz fork by applying the point or the side of the stem. In no time at all you will feel the knot release.

Cramps
Place the side of the stem on the muscle and roll it back and forth over the area. This will help the muscle to relax. Michael's oil mixed with equal amounts of Shekinah oil will work wonders with calming the cramping muscle.

Shoulder Pain
From muscle strain of over working or too much typing the 50 Hz can be used by running the stem point over the area where it hurts. You should start to feel the endorphins being released along with the pain and stiffness subsiding.

Carpel Tunnel and Sciatica
Using the stem point, run it down the pain line slowly. You will have to vibrate the fork several times to sent the vibrations down the entire length of the pain line. Again you may want to use Michael's oil and the Shekinah oil.

Numbness
For numbness, take the stem and place it on the area. I have found that the oil of Gabriel works well in this process because of its gentleness and healing qualities. Constricted nerves should open rather easily, however, severely damaged nerves will take more time to repair themselves. In either case repeat the tuning process until feeling returns.

The Psychic Fork Set

The Psychic Fork Set is a set of 5 forks that are set to the brain waves of someone who is proficient in these gifts. Each of us possesses these gifts, even if we do not use them or are even aware of them. These frequencies are used to tune your brain to the frequencies of having these psychic gifts. Some have experiences immediately while others have to continue to practice and have patience. Be open to allowing yourself to come to these frequencies within your own being. The forks work very well with the CD set, because you have the best of both worlds - the meditating process and the actual vibrations being placed on the areas to be tuned.

Kundalini Brain Wave

The Kundalini tuning fork holds the same frequency as that of a Master passing this energy or the person receiving the experiencing of it. Kundalini can be thought of as a rich source of psychic or libidinous energy in our unconscious. This energy can be used to heighten the spiritual experience or the sexual experience and then again both. It is the energy of creation and it is this energy you tap into whenever you are manifesting anything. This tuning fork has been designed in its frequency to stimulate the flow of Kundalini energy.

INSTRUCTIONS:
The first thing you will need to do is center yourself; reach that place in meditation of allowance, where you let go of all judgments and just open yourself to receive. Pinch the weighted ends together and quickly slide your fingers away letting the prongs of the tuning fork vibrate. As the tuning fork vibrates place it on the base of the spine where it meets the skull. The point of the fork should be in the soft tissue just below the skull with the stem of the fork resting against the base of the skull. You may need to pinch the ends together several times to keep the vibration going to carry the frequency to the brain. For those of you that have received "shaktipat" before, you will notice how quickly the experience returns. For those of you that have not I can tell you this, Shakti is the equivalent to a combined physical and spiritual orgasm, without an ejaculation and can last hours.

Third Eye Brain Wave

This tuning fork is set to the brain waves of a fully functioning and focused third eye. This is designed to help those that have not been able to use their third eye to do so. As the brain waves are reproduced in the brain you will be able to start training your third eye to see clearly. Colors will become more rich and vibrant and you will be able to see energies from things with your eyes closed. As you become proficient in third eye work with your eyes closed, you will reach a point where you can see auras with your eyes open. You will be able to look into a body and see things that are out in the way of diseases.

INSTRUCTIONS:

The first thing you will need to do is center yourself, reach that place in meditation of allowance, where you let go of all judgments and just open yourself to receive. Pinch the weighted ends together and quickly slide your fingers away letting the prongs of the tuning fork vibrate. Place the tuning fork just above the third eye, which is located in the center of your forehead. Close your physical eyes and notice what you see. Most people see black; so don't get discouraged if that is what you see. Bring to mind a color, preferably a sky blue emanating in the area of the third eye. As you begin to see this color you will notice it begins to fill all that you are seeing. You may have to vibrate the tuning fork several times as the vibration lessens. When you can see a sky blue color you are now ready to bring to mind other colors. After you master the colors, you can start focusing on different objects and people with your third eye. When that is mastered and you can use your third eye to see color and objects, you are well on your way to seeing auras. Continue to practice until you become proficient at seeing auras and then you can begin to look inside bodies for things that are out.

Total Knowing Brain Wave

Total knowing comes from another realm of awareness. This tuning fork is designed to get you to that realm of knowing. Most people operate in only two realms of knowing. The first realm is "I know I know". This is very helpful to us as it is from this knowing we go about our lives. We do the work we know how to do. We run a family in the way we know works. We do the same with choosing our friends or buying the things we need in our lives to be happy. The second realm is "I know I don't know". This is helpful in our lives, because if we know we don't know; we can learn. We can get the education we need to get the promotion at work. We can learn better ways to participate with our families where everyone feels loved and empowered. When we read instructions to fix or put something together we are operation in this realm.

The third realm is "I don't know I don't know". This is the realm of self- discovery that is very helpful in the growth process of a person. As teenagers we are all geniuses that can't understand how our mother and father ever made it this far being as stupid as they are. We know all there is to know or think we do. When we mature in life we begin to know that there are many thing we didn't know we didn't know.

The fourth realm is " I don't know I know". This happens when we have an epiphany or what is called an "A Ha" moment. These are not the times when we read it or someone told us what to think. Oh, no. These are the times when we are able to reach into the brain wave patterns that allow us to draw on total knowing. Not as an understanding of it but a natural knowing of a universal truth.

INSTRUCTIONS:

The first thing you will need to do is center yourself; reach that place in meditation of allowance, where you let go of all judgments and just open yourself to receive. Pinch the weighted ends together and quickly slide your fingers away letting the prongs of the tuning fork vibrate. For this tuning you will need to alternate from one side of the forehead to the other beginning with the left side. Place the point or the stem of the fork along the hairline in the corners of the forehead, directly above the temples. We are activating the brain wave in the frontal lobes. As these brain waves change and the brain begins to become accustom to operating at this frequency you will start having A Ha's. Things that have not been working in your life for sometime will start opening up to you. There will be solutions to problems that you never thought of before profoundly changing the way you think about life and you in it.

P.S.I. Brain Wave

This psychic tuning fork is designed to raise your level of psychic ability. The brain waves are set to enhance your perception far beyond just a good guess. When you can train your brain to use these waves you will be able to use the psychic gifts that are innate in all of us. It has been said we only use 10% of our brains true power. This 10% has nothing to do with how smart someone is. This has everything to do with how much of the gray matter is operating at any given time. The more of the brain that is being used the more we are aware of The more we can tap into the better we are in having the happy lives we want.

INSTRUCTIONS:
The first thing you will need to do is center yourself; reach that place in meditation of allowance, where you let go of all judgments and just open yourself to receive. Pinch the weighted ends together and quickly slide your fingers away letting the prongs of the tuning fork vibrate. For this tuning you will need to alternate from one side of the forehead to the other, beginning with the left side. Place the point or the stem of the fork along the hairline in the corners of the forehead, directly above the temples. We are activating the brain waves in the frontal lobes. As you tune your brain to these frequencies the more you will be able to pick up when working with other people. The more you will be able to pick up in your life and what is going on around you. Your ability to avoid situations that could lead to trouble will increase vastly along with you being able to take advantage of situations for your benefit. Lastly as you reach the place where you master the use of these brain waves there comes the ability to move objects.

Change Matter Brain Waves

This tuning fork is designed to take the brain waves to a much higher level. It is from these brain waves that very few people can alter mater. There is a catch with these brain waves. Which is simply this, unless you have mastered the lower frequencies and can come into these brain waves with a complete benevolent and loving body, mind, and soul combined you will not be able to change matter. The good news is if you can master the lower levels to get you to this point you will be in that place of love.

INSTRUCTIONS:
The first thing you will need to do is center yourself; reach that place in meditation of allowance, where you let go of all judgments and just open yourself to receive. Pinch the weighted ends together and quickly slide your fingers away letting the prongs of the tuning fork vibrate. For this tuning you will need to alternate from one side of the forehead to the other, beginning with the left side. Place the point or the stem of the fork along the hairline in the corners of the forehead, directly above the temples. We are activating the brain waves in the frontal lobes. You will know when you get there.

Transmutation Brain Wave
Creation or Creation 2

This tuning fork is the frequency of the very structure of the DNA vibration. We call it the Creation fork (sold separately from the set). Scientists are using this frequency to rejuvenate and repair DNA. What they have been able to accomplish with it is nothing to what you can do if you can tune your brain waves to this frequency.

INSTRUCTIONS:
The first thing you will need to do is center yourself; reach that place in meditation of allowance, where you let go of all judgments and just open yourself to receive. The Creation tuning fork is either weighted or not, so you will need to tap the prongs on something made of hard rubber to get it vibrating or pinch the prongs together if weighted. For this tuning you will need to alternate from one side of the forehead to the other, beginning with the left side. Place the point or the stem of the fork along the hairline in the corners of the forehead, directly above the temples. We are activating the brain waves in the frontal lobes. You will know when you get there.

Astral/Mental Projection Wave

This tuning fork (not included in the set) is the frequency of conscious thoughts. These are the thoughts you are aware of having or that you intentionally put your mind too. This makes this frequency great for improving your ability to communicate with others. You can focus on mentally projecting your thoughts to another so they understand what it is that you are saying. For the most part we do not think in words but pictures. It can also be used to astrally project your Higher Self for travel in the astral realm for self-discovery and learning.

INSTRUCTIONS:

The first thing you will need to do is center yourself; reach that place in meditation of allowance, where you let go of all judgments and just open yourself to receive. The Astral/Mental tuning fork is weighted so pinch the prongs together to get it vibrating. For this tuning you will need to place the fork on the crown and then both of the temples, alternate from one side of the forehead to the other. We are activating the brain waves in the frontal lobes. You will know when you get there.

Standard Chakra Set

Tuned to the vibrations of the chakras. The handles are color coded to make them easier to use in chakra alignments and Crystaline reiki sessions

Tree of Life Tuning Forks

This awesome set includes the Sacred Solfeggio scale. They are used in conjunction with the chakra forks in healing. This set includes 11 forks, each imprinted with the angels' names and color coded for easy identification. Each fork has a different use in healing from correcting DNA to rejuvenating cells.

Sefirot Tuning Forks

The Sefirot tuning forks are a set of 11 forks that are used for attuning the angelic forks in the Tree of Life set. Each Sefirot has a frequency with a numerical value that equals three, six or nine the same as the Tree of Life set.

Creation Frequency

This fork is combined with the others to cause things to happen or to create things. It can be used alone or with the Gabriel fork to repair damaged portions of DNA. It can also be used alone or with the Shekinah fork to destroy cancer cells. It also will move bones and joints back into place when they are out of alignment. It will also repair and rebuild muscles and tissue. These are just a few of the amazing things we are discovering about this frequency the possibilities are endless.

Circulation Fork

The frequency of the Circulation fork is used to stimulate the flow of blood to areas of the body. Arthritis is a prime example of poor circulation in the joints. Once the flow of blood is returned to the damaged areas it will start to heal its self. The Circulation forks frequency works on Diabetes and other diseases, as well.

To use the Circulation fork simply start it vibrating by tapping it on the heal of the hand. Once it is vibrating place the tip of the stem/handle on the joint or area where there is stiffness or pain. Allow the tuning fork tip to remain on the area until it stops vibrating and then repeat the process three to four more times. Massaging or vigorously rubbing the area helps to spread the frequency vibration especially applying Michael's oil when massaging the area.

With diabetes you will want to cover as much area as possible. The process is the same for vibrating the fork and placement. However, you will need to work in areas about 10 inches apart. Pick an area where you want to stimulate blood flow and place the stem tip on there. Let the fork vibrate until it stops. Do this 3 to 4 times before moving on to another area. You may then massage the area you just worked on or massage all of the areas when you have finished with the fork. You may do this process several times during the day for faster results but it is not necessary. Once a week will help in restoring the flow of blood to the areas but it will take longer to have the desired results.

This frequency has also been found to reduce cholesterol. Simply start the fork vibrating and place over the area of the liver.

Psychic Set

The psychic set of tuning forks can be used to enhance one's intuitive and psychic abilities, those forks consists of the PSI fork, at 252.20 hertz, the change matter fork at 351.20 hertz, the total knowing fork at 108.40 herta, the third eye fork at 82.80 hertz and the Kundalini fork at 55.60 hertz. Using these specific forks, after balancing the chakras can stimulate the individual into experiencing a state of enhanced psychic abilities, which can be come permeate if used over a specific time frame in the manner layout in the Psychic set manual.

Afterthoughts- 2023

The healing art of sound healing with tuning forks has gone through a lot of changes, research and expansion since I start working as a certified Tuning Fork Practitioner in 2001.I still use tuning forks in my healing practice, and teach the art of tuning fork healing and how to use it with other modalities, such as massage, Reiki. Crystal and Gemstone Healing, Intuitive Healing,and Spititual Healing.

I have even worked with Chiropractors who have used tuning forks in their healing practice, as well as Acupuncturists who have used them in their healing practice. Tuning forks are part of Vibrational Medicine and will hopefully be embraced by holistic healthcare providers as well as mainstream medical care providers, to provide for the best care for their clients/patients.

As people become aware of how to utilize tuning forks in their own self care, we will all become healthier and more balanced in our journey called life.

The future holds promising research possibilities for tuning forks and their use in the healing of people and animals.

If you enjoy this book, perhaps you will enjoy reading some of my other books as well:

Quantum Healing: The synergy of Chiropractic and Reiki, co-authored with Dr. Pat Doughtery, D.C.

Advanced Sound Healing with Tuning Forks

Atlantean Reiki: Healing Knowledge from a lost civilization

Crystal Reiki Workbook

Crystaline Reiki: A New Frequency of Healing

Crystal & Gemstone Healing: Using Using Crystals and Gemstones in the art of Healing

Medical Intuition Handbook: An Overview of Medical Intuition, its history and famous Medical :Intuitive's of the World

Vibrational Yoga: Using Voice Sounds in the Yogic Experience

Upcoming Books:
                By Charles Lightwalker

Medical Intuition and Muscle Testing Co-Authored with Dr. Pat Doughtery

Life Changing Lesson from an Elder: Learning the Metis Medicine Ways Co-Authored with Charles Edwards, Ph.D.

Musings: A collection of Poetry, Writings & Thoughts

Bits and Pieces :A collection of philosophy according to Charles Lightwalker

Learning to Channel Workbook

Charles is a member of the following professional organizations:

- International Association of Medical Intuitives
- Natural Healers Association
- International Holistic Therapies Directory
- Natural Health Resource Alliance
- Spiritual Healers and Earth Stewards
- The Metaphysical Research Society
- Alternative Healthcare Alliance/Spokane
- Sound Healers Of Washington
- International Association of Healthcare Practitioners
- American Holistic Health Association
- Sound Healer Association
- World Reiki Association
- International Association of Sound healers
- Society for Shamanic Practitioners
- National Federation of Spiritual Healers (U.K.)

The History of Sound Healing and the use of Tuning Forks in Theraputic Sound Healing

By *Charles Lightwalker*

In 1550 in Pavia, Italy, Girolamo Cardano, a physician, mathematician and astrologer, noticed how sound was being perceived through the skin. In 1553 in Padua, Italy, H. Capivacci, a physician, noticed that this knowledge of sound being perceived through the skin might be used as a diagnostic tool for differentiating between hearing disorders located in the middle ear or in the acoustic nerve. In 1684, German physician G. C. Schelhammer tried using a common cutlery fork to enhance the experiments that Cardano and Capivacci were working on. In 1711 in England, Royal trumpeter and luteist, John Shore, created the first tuning fork. At that time, he lovingly and jokingly called it a pitch fork. It was made of steel and had a pitch of A423.5. In 1800, German physicist E.F.F. Chladni, along with others, constructed a complete musical instrument based on sets of tuning forks. In 1834, J.H. Scheibler presented a set of 54 tuning forks covering ranges from 220 Hz to 440Hz. Later, in Paris, J. Lissajous constructed a tuning fork with a resonance box. Also in Paris, German physicist K. R. Koening invented a tuning fork, which was kept in continuous vibration by a clockwork. In 1863 in Heidelberg, physiologist H. Helmholtz, used sets of electromagnetically powered tuning forks for his experiments on the sensations of tone. Tuning forks were indispensible instruments for producing defined sinusoidal vibrations and used as a diagnostic tool in otology. The most common system of determining the pitch of all twelve notes in a octave is the Equal temperament. The standard pitch here is A440. As a side note, equal temperament was proposed by Aristoxenus, a pupil of Aristotle, and had been in use in China for some centuries. Mr. Hipkins, the head piano tuner in 1846, was instructed by

Walter Broadwood to instruct his piano tuners in the use of equal temperament. To do this, he used two tuning forks; one for meantone at A433.5 and one for equal temperament at A436. Even though musicians were among the first people to work with pitch, scientist enjoyed sharing knowledge and use of the tuning fork also. As far back as 583 BC, when the Greek philosopher, Pythagorus, made a device called the monochord and set the pitch to 256Hz.. The Egyptians and Greeks used the monochord to make intricate mathematical calculations. It wasn't until around 1834 when a group of German physicists was able to use a mechanical stroboscopic device, that they were able to determine that the pitch of the tuning fork was at A440cps (which later was expressed as A440Hz). Even though the pitch of the note "A" in the 17th century varied from 373.3 Hz to 402.0 Hz, on July 27, 1987, the International society of Piano Builders and Technicians unanimously support A=440 Hz. as the international pitch standard for piano manufacturers and for modern piano and orchestral tuning.

WHO USES TUNING FORKS IN SOUND HEALING

By *Charles Lightwalker*

Everyday people and practitioners in the Healing Arts are using tuning forks to positively alter the body's biochemistry. Sound enhances the healing effects of all energy therapy practices.

People who use tuning forks are often involved with:

- Acupuncturists
- Chiropractors
- Polarity Therapy
- Crystaline Reiki Therapy
- Massage Therapy
- Yoga Therapy
- Hypnotherapy
- Psychotherapy
- Meditation
- Reflexology
- Shamanic Healing

And anyone interested in alternative healing modalities and pain management. You can use tuning forks and sound to experience deep levels of healing by bringing your body back to its fundamental pulse and by connecting you to your Core Rhythm.

Why are so many people using Tuning Forks?

- Provides instantaneous, deep state of relaxation
- Improves mental clarity and brain functioning
- Increases your level of physical energy and mental concentration (Energy Fork)
- Relieves stress by drawing your body into a centered space

- Enhances massage, acupressure, dream-work and meditation
- Brings your nervous system into balance (Nerve fork)
- Integrates left and right brain thought patterns
- Increase psychic abilities (Psychic Set)

When you tap the tuning forks, you awaken the life energy of your cells and start them puffing, creating a centered, happy feeling inside. Align your body and mind with the world's best sound healing technologies.

With tuning forks you'll be able to:

- Achieve deep relaxation and mind/body balance in seconds--not hours
- Reduce stress and muscular tension, spasms and pain nearly instantaneously (Nerve Fork)
- Increase blood flow and circulation by releasing constriction around targeted organs (Circulation fork)
- Transcend to higher levels of consciousness and access spiritual insights (Creation Fork)

Each tuning fork is calibrated at a specific frequency to address different areas of healing and development.

Six Sound Healing Facts to Consider
By Charles Lightwalker

Sound healing with tuning forks can be combined with other complimentary care healing modalities, such as chiropratic, crystal and Gemstone healing, massage therapy, Reiki healing, Shamanic healing, and yoga to enhance overall balance and healing for the client.
Here is six facts to consider about Sound Healing.
*Instruments: Various instruments like tuning forks, crystal bowls, Tibetan singing bowls, gongs, and even the human voice can be used in sound healing.
*Frequency Matters: Different sound frequencies interact differently with the body's energy (auric) fields.
*Binaural Beats: Binaural beats are a type of sound wave therapy that uses different frequencies tones in each ear, which are then processed by the brain into a single beat. This healing method said to induce states of relaxation, focus, or creativity depending on the frequency used.
*Brainwave Entrainment: Brainwave entrainment involves synchronizing brain wave frequencies to specific rhythms. This has been used to alter mental states, improve focus, or promote relaxation.
*Chakra Alignment: There are twelve Chakras-Energy Centers, each resonating with a specific frequency. Tuning Fork Practitioner use specific scientificllu calibrated tuning forks to balance these energy centers promoting physical, emotional, mental well being.
*Stess Reduction: Sound healing can promote deep states of relaxation and stress reduction.

List of Sound Healing
Tuning Fork Books References

Advanced Sound Healing with Tuning Forks, C.Lightwalker

Healing Sounds, J. Goldman

Stem Cells, Dr. Joe Crain

Acutuning 1,& 2, Dr. Joe Crain

Tuning Fork Therapy F. Milford

Opening the Psychic Pathways, C. Lightwalker

The Healing Power of Sound, M. Gaynor,M.D.

The Cosmic Octave, Hans Cousto

This by no means a complete list of excellent books on Sound healing. More books are listed in my advanced book.

Milton Keynes UK
Ingram Content Group UK Ltd.
UKHW041454121024
449426UK00001B/95

9 781835 380741

Fun Spirituality

Vladimir Živković

Published by Vladimir Živković, 2024.

FUN SPIRITUALITY
"Exposure of Contemporary Misconceptions of Science, Atheism, Religion, Philosophy and Spirituality"
Živković Vladimir
Smashwords Edition
Copyright 2024

While every precaution has been taken in the preparation of this book, the publisher assumes no responsibility for errors or omissions, or for damages resulting from the use of the information contained herein.

FUN SPIRITUALITY

First edition. October 11, 2024.

Copyright © 2024 Vladimir Živković.

ISBN: 979-8227266002

Written by Vladimir Živković.

CONTENT

CONTENT..
INTRODUCTION..
GOD'S CREATION..

   IN WHAT WAY IS GOD WITHIN US?
   GOD IS A MIRROR
   SPIRITUAL AND PHYSICAL LAWS
   CONSCIOUSNESS AND MIND
   FREE WILL
   FREEDOM (explanation of God's vision and our task)
   GOD IS NOT ENERGY
   INFINITE COSMOS?

MEN AND WOMEN..

   A NUISANCES OF VICE
   EVIL OF SEDUCTION
   IGNORING PEOPLE AND DOING EVIL
   IMPOSING THE WILL
   CHANGES

SCIENTIFIC MANIPULATIONS.........................

   DENIAL OF SELF AND EXPERIENCE (logic and knowledge)
   FAITH IN EVIDENCE
   WHAT IS EVOLUTION AND WHAT IS CREATIONISM?
   EVOLUTION AGAINST THE THEORY OF EVOLUTION
   SIMPLE MATH
   WHICH IS BETTER?

RELIGION AND FAITH

BAD DEFINITION OF FAITH (or belief, it's the same for me)
FAITH IN GOD IS PRIMARY KNOWLEDGE
SPIRITUAL TEACHINGS
FAITH AND KNOWLEDGE
TRANSIENT RELIGION
HOW TO FIND GOD?

PHILOSOPHICAL ERRORS

CONSCIOUSNESS AND THE EGOCENTRIC MIND
THE WATCHMAKER ANALOGY
THE BEGINNING OF LOGIC
BURDEN OF PROOF
RULE OF EVIDENCE
FRAUDULENCE OF FACTS AND EVIDENCE
FALLACY
PHILOSOPHY AS IGNORANCE
LET'S BE RATIONAL

ATHEISM AS DOUBT AND IGNORANCE

MY WORK
ATHEISM IS NOT A LACK OF FAITH IN GOD
EVIDENCE OR PROOF OF GOD
DEAF–MUMBLED GOD
BAD FAITH
DEMAND OF ATHEISTS FOR EVIDENCE OF GOD
ATHEISTIC "CRITICAL THINKING"
ATHEISM IS FALSE LOGIC
ATHEISTIC DOUBT

ATHEISM AS IGNORANCE HAS NO DEBATE
WHY ATHEISTS DO NOT KNOW GOD?
ATHEISM IS IGNORANCE
HOW?
EXIT FROM IGNORANCE
ATHEISM AND JESUS
SOURCE
ATHEISTIC "CRITICAL THINKING" HAS NO KNOWLEDGE
PREJUDICES OF ATHEISM
ATHEISM HAS NO FAITH IN SELF AND EXPERIENCE

SPIRITUAL EGO..

A SEA OF MISUNDERSTANDING
BE A WISE SNAKE THAT DOES NOT BITE
KNOWLEDGE AND OPINION
DOGMA TOWARDS ONESELF
PICTURE
VISION OF GOD
SPIRITUAL EDUCATION
JUDGMENT OR COMMON SENSE?

FOOD FOR PHILOSOPHERS...

LYING?
UNIVERSE AS EVIDENCE
EVIDENCE OF GOD
WHEN WILL WE GET FREE OF IGNORANCE AND TRICKS?
FOOD FOR THE MIND

WE FIGHT FOR THE POSITIVE TRANSFORMATION OF CHRISTIANITY..

JESUS' WORK AND TEACHING ARE PERFECT
JUDAS IS A BELIEVER JUST LIKE ANY OTHER
CHRISTIAN DISAGREEMENTS (or, social and religious issues)

INTRODUCTION

TODAY, EVERYONE WILL tell you that you have the right to believe, think and do what you want.

I can say that you have that right only if you do good deeds. Otherwise, bad deeds affect other people who also have free will like you. If you affect the free will of other people negatively, then the consequences of your free will will also be negative and you will not be able to choose.

As we can see, declaring that you can believe and do whatever you want is not productive and throws you into slavery and unhappiness. The people who preach this are not good people, but are false saints, they show false goodness and false knowledge.

Why did I write this book?

In the modern age, there is a breakthrough of science and, therefore, of atheism. The modern philosophy of science and atheism is not good for the spiritual development of man. And the spiritual development of a person is the most important thing. Spiritual development brings the development of consciousness, the ability for love and happiness, the path to freedom and faith in a better tomorrow.

Science and atheism lead you to a false world, false knowledge, despair and unhappiness. These people try to convince you that everything is accidental and that life has no meaning by forcing you to live this life selfishly without considering the consequences. They want to convince you that life for a moment and only this life is valuable.

However, without God, spiritual development and the meaning of life, everything is barren and worthless. Such a life is worthless.

You will notice in this book that I am extremely opposed to the implementation of scientific methods and atheistic philosophy through human life. Such a lifestyle robs people of happiness and dignity, and does not value personal life and personal experience and knowledge. It is the manipulation of a mediocre mind to live for impulses and false intelligence and not for yourself.

This book will surprise you with incredible revelations of delusions among the most intelligent circles. If you want real arguments and knowledge for every kind of debate and philosophy of life, this is the book for you.

Through this book, I want every reader to recognize the ignorance and manipulation of science, philosophy, religion, atheism, and false spirituality, because only the recognition of delusions and a return to the true life and spiritual path can heal the world and society.

Good luck everyone! Prosperity and peace!

GOD'S CREATION

IN WHAT WAY IS GOD WITHIN US?

I recently read a statement by Rumi that reads:
– You are not a drop in the ocean. You are an entire ocean in a single drop.

What does that mean?

The author of the statement wanted to emphasize that the total God dwells in us. In this way, it is emphasized that the whole universe is inside us.

This statement is not far from the truth, however, the error is in the first statement of this statement. And that is, that it is not true that you are not a drop in the ocean. If the entire ocean is contained in one drop, then the drop is also contained in the ocean.

In order to better understand this, we will say the statement that man is God, but God is not just that man.

This statement already seems more logical and understandable. We cannot say man is not God, but God is man. That would mean that man is older than God, and then God would have to be only man, and that is not true.

I also recently read a text where someone on the Internet asked for help with a solution to a math problem. Since no one came forward to help, he logged in with another account and wrote the wrong solution in the comments. As he wrote it, many people came forward to correct him and give the correct solution.

The idea is that people like to correct rather than help.

Maybe that's largely true, but it's impossible that no one wants to help. If that were really the case, there would be no help for us.

Someone wrote that 10% of people are good, 10% of people are evil, and 80% are in the middle with variations. This means that 10% of people are driving the progress of mankind from the beginning of the world until today. That is why revolutionary discoveries are dedicated to that ten percent of good humanity, because they are the only ones capable of putting modern values into practice.

So don't be disappointed by other people's misunderstanding. If out of 10 people you find one person who understands you, then you are more than understandable enough. The problem is if a lot of people understand you. Then you're not doing anything sensible.

The lesson is:

That's how God created the world. A little good brings great progress. God swallows a lot of evil without a problem. The world will never be destroyed. Unfortunately, there will be no apocalypse today, or tomorrow. These are all fabrications of a complexed mind eager for liberation from the suffering of evil and despair.

However, suffering is an integral part of life, and it will never go away. Not even when you realize the Self. It is God who endures the suffering of the whole world. It just seems to be us.

Therefore it is correct to say:

You are a drop in the ocean that has the same essence as the ocean itself. The realization of that essence will make you an ocean, ie. realized God.

That's the goal, and that's the truth.

Of course, there is a possibility that Rumi's statement is not well translated.

He probably said:

– You are not just a drop in the ocean. You are the entire ocean in that single drop.

GOD IS A MIRROR

A person who is on the spiritual path constantly has problems and troubles. While solving these problems, he/she constantly thinks of God because spirituality includes God necessarily.

When somebody thinks of God when he/she has problems, those problems can make him/her think that God is like this or like that. Thoughts like temptation that God is unjust and unforgiving can preoccupy a spiritual aspirant.

When something like this happens to you, remember the law that your opinion about God and what you see in God is an opinion about yourself. The flaws you see in God are yours.

Of course, you should not take this literally but cognitively.

More precisely, your opinion of God is a guide to what you might usefully change and do.

Atheists who claim that God does not exist in reality consider themselves non-existent. They have a destructive and desperate belief that they will cease to exist. A man who considers God unjust is probably unjust and unforgiving himself.

Some people say that if God exists, then God is a murderer, rapist, pedophile, manipulator, narcissist...to name a few.

Beware of such people. These are people who have such qualities but hide behind their opinion about God, which in reality is subconscious knowledge of themselves and their flaws.

The lesson is:

Let your opinion about God be a guideline for your own change for the better, so that when you don't know what is happening to you and why, you can find positive actions in yourself that you will put into action.

SPIRITUAL AND PHYSICAL LAWS

Science mainly studies physical laws.

Psychology is one branch of science that would have to include God. This is because the only psychic healing is found in knowing who you are, who God is, that God is and that we are searching for Self and God.

A psychology that does not have these answers has nothing to treat correctly.

That's why Freud found only improvements and progress but not a solution (because he threw out the solution at the start as an impossible solution). His disillusionment and intolerance towards religion is to blame for this.

Spiritual laws are different from physical laws. Physical laws are at the service of spiritual ones, and spiritual laws are at the service of God.

One of the most important spiritual laws is the law of karma and reincarnation.

Physical laws are karma on the physical level. Spiritual laws are karma on the spiritual level. This means that all living things get the fate they deserve to the last millimeter. God is so omnipotent that every being lives his karma in relation to others.

One may consider spiritual laws to be non-existent because they are "invisible". However, neither God nor karma are invisible but recognizable.

With the expansion of consciousness and the strengthening of virtues, everything spiritual becomes visible because virtue is what God believes. God trusts a man with virtue. More precisely, God does not think about trust because God is omniscient and gives man in a second all the good things he deserves.

Why is this good?

Because you are aware that God's gift and recognition is something you deserve. It gives you a sense of self-worth.

That is why the realization of one's own and other people's value is also God.

CONSCIOUSNESS AND MIND

Our acquired consciousness never declines.
Why?

Because we suffered to deserve it. A person mostly deserves mercy, love and compassion through a difficult fate. The difficulties you have overcome must be justly repaid. No one suffers in vain.

On the other hand, acquired wisdom can be lost. Some people think it is wise or reasonable to exclude God from reality. In this way, a person does not become smarter.

FREE WILL

Self–refuting claim:

"Let people do what they want," said a man who believes that everyone has the right to do what they want.

Me:

– Then why are you bothering me if everyone has the right to do what they want?

"Freedom is to do good".

Question:

–Does a person really have the right to do what he wants?

Many say that their life is their business.

Is that really so?

If we start from the fact that even thoughts are negative or positive energy directed at the object of the thought, does this mean that nothing is just our business?

Conclusion:

– Not everyone does as he wants, but as he can.

This is proof of free will.

How?

Free will is exercised in the world and in life. The world does not adapt to the free will of the individual.

Your actions based on your free will determine what you can and cannot do at a given moment.

This is great because it reveals God's law that no one can take away what you deserve.

It is the grace and justice of human free will.

FREEDOM (EXPLANATION of God's vision and our task)

The task that God the Creator gave us is very simple we just have to accept it.

People tend to ask:

Why did God put us in trouble if he is so good and loving? Why didn't he give us freedom right away?

The answers are simple:

Creation is perfect because it is real and just and has the perfect task of giving us full self–awareness through experience and our free will. So, we choose what we will do, but the consequences are determined by God, that is. karma. Based on that, we gain self–awareness (which is the basic task of Creation). Therefore, nature does not select anything but the needs of the soul's consciousness.

Gaining full self–awareness is our full freedom and happiness and then God's enrichment.

I adore Jesus who said he would sit on the throne next to our God the father. And he said that each of us will carry our cross (live and work out karma) until the end of time (liberation – complete self–awareness).

Here I want to emphasize that atheism is the only belief that does not preach freedom. True knowledge must preach freedom. Otherwise, everything is meaningless and not worth a fleeting life. Atheism is the only belief that does not understand that happiness is not found in fleeting life and enjoyment. Freedom in the transient does not exist if you are not aware of the goal.

Why am I saying this?

Because of the new worship of science, intelligence is at a premium. However, what does that intelligence give? Does it give freedom? No. Then it is not real knowledge.

The lesson is:

–True knowledge gives us optimism and happiness because that knowledge of God and freedom makes us safe and accessible, and in this way we willingly face challenges because we understand that these challenges lead us to a perfect goal.

That is why God threw us into trouble. To have a real life and a real goal.

It is important that you understand that every trouble and every life will have an end, only you together with God will not.

So, you can already relax and work on yourself happily or at least willingly.

GOD IS NOT ENERGY

Many clergy today say that God is energy and that we are energy. Some even say that the Universe is one big ocean of energy.

That is not true.

Just as man can identify with body or mind, he also identifies with energy.

Many people even say that everything is energy without even having experienced the subtle and astral worlds.

God is neither physical nor energy. It is all reality (illusion) that God creates.

Because God is the Self of all creation and all living beings, and has no appearance, no form, no smell, no taste, people equate such a description with nothingness.

Yet God is not nothing. God is an all–powerful impersonal entity that can be experienced and known. God is the all–powerful source from which all that God wills comes forth. And everything is perfect.

INFINITE COSMOS?

Here are the simple facts.

Scientists claim that energy can neither be created nor destroyed. So, this is another paradox, because in order for energy to exist it must be created. Such energy was created by God, ensuring the self–sustainability of the Cosmos.

However, here too, people fall into the delusion of thinking that the Cosmos is self-sustaining because of self–sustaining energy. This is not true. This self–sustainability of energy was made possible by God as the Self. This means that if God separated himself from the energy, the energy would disappear.

MEN AND WOMEN

A NUISANCES OF VICE

In the course of my life, I have witnessed the degradation of women many times.

Female decay begins when an unprepared woman enters into an emotional relationship with a man who disappoints her. When she experiences disappointment, a woman becomes susceptible to many vices. Vices destroy human dignity.

A woman becomes unfaithful without even noticing it.

She starts drinking alcohol and smoking cigarettes and living in bad company. It cannot be avoided because today it is fashionable to go out to exclusive places where every vice is present.

A penchant for love relationships creates promiscuity because relationships are increasingly weak and unstable and short-lived.

If such a woman meets a better man, she will not be able to establish a good relationship with him because there are vices, bad company and bad behavior that create insurmountable problems.

So in the end it happens that a woman has to accept a man who is the same as her. Wicked and unfaithful.

Here they seem to be a good couple because they are blind to other people's flaws because they want to cover up or justify their own.

This is where big problems and big injuries come later, because flaws are always flaws.

Thus, every woman ends up regretting missed opportunities. And that's because it simply doesn't repair its flaws. More precisely, a woman does not try to love herself and correct herself, but looks for an accomplice in misfortune.

And the accomplice in her misfortune is her greatest enemy, whom she naively classifies as a friend at first. That is why the most common explanation of women is that her man was good at first and then changed.

The lesson is:

If you change yourself for the better, you will not only be happier, but you will also get a better future.

Don't believe in random luck. Fight for yourself and your love the right way. God is with you.

EVIL OF SEDUCTION

Hell is only found on Earth.

However, selfish and evil people think that Hell is somewhere else.

Why?

They haven't experienced suffering of the heart.

When you chase after money and genitals, only ego injuries occur.

Ego injuries are easy to heal. You just get up, shake off the dust, and look for a new victim.

IGNORING PEOPLE AND DOING EVIL

A man is not an appendix that you can cut out.

What does that mean?

If you have done harm to someone, it is logical that you want to avoid that person and the consequences.

What are people doing today?

They do evil and then employ people to cover up that evil. At the same time, they involve other people without respecting the personality of those people. If you hurt one person and ran away, you do the same to a new person.

In this way, a karmic burden is created that manifests as a living hell.

The lesson is:

When the karmic ball is unwound, both the righteous and the unrighteous suffer greatly.

A righteous man is healed and freed. An unrighteous man becomes sick and enslaved by his wrongdoings.

An unjust and unfaithful man meets worse and worse people and stays in an eternally bad society and is overtaken by infidelity and crime.

IMPOSING THE WILL

The imposition of will is not always negative.

Without the imposition of will, there would be no progress.

If parents prevent their children from smoking cigarettes, it is imposing will, but it is not negative.

When children get rid of their parents, they can feel relieved because now they can smoke without anyone objecting to them.

Over time, they begin to miss precisely this imposition of will.

Every coin has two faces.

It is never about imposing will but about right and wrong.

Opposing another's right will is in large part an exercise of one's own negative will.

Like, say, smoking cigarettes.

Are you saying it's the smoker's business and nobody else's business?

CHANGES

The best life changes happen gradually, with understanding.

What does that mean?

When it comes to love partners, your partner is a very good mirror.

In the modern era, good conclusions have been reached that you should take care of your partner, his/her wishes and his/her individuality.

However, for a marriage or relationship to survive, we must take care of our partner or it will end.

That's why people make sacrifices for their partner. However, if you think that you are sacrificing yourself for your partner, there is a high probability that there will be problems.

How and why?

Feelings and circumstances are changeable in nature. If you are angry with your partner, in those moments you will stop doing the good you were doing for him/her. In this way, the positive changes you adopted because of your partner lose their result and meaning. Because you did positive things for him/her and not for yourself and not because it was right.

What does this mean next?

You have to carefully consider and understand the changes that your partner wants you to make. If your partner's complaint is positive and justified, you will implement the change best if you understand it for your own good, and only then for your partner's.

The lesson is:

A huge percentage of divorce shows that people do not understand the sacrifice and care for the partner. If you commit evil and vices, such as infidelity, smoking and alcohol, no amount of sacrifice and care for your partner on the other side will fix the situation.

You have to be a good man for your own good. Only then will you be good to others.

At this point we understand our saying:

He who is not good for himself is not good for others either.

Many understand this saying in the wrong context of selfishness and ego. Yet you are not the ego.

More natural:

Stop thinking that you are sacrificing yourself for your partner.

SCIENTIFIC MANIPULATIONS
DENIAL OF SELF AND EXPERIENCE (logic and knowledge)

Let's consider that I ate. Based on my experience, I can claim what I ate and how the food tasted.

Some people will ask me for proof that I ate.

There are probably methods that can prove what I ate, but those methods cannot prove for sure how the food was prepared, how I ate it and what it tasted like, etc...

Also, that evidence can be planted and processed arbitrarily.

Many people realize that there are evidences and facts in nature. However, the processing and understanding of the facts themselves can be biased and inaccurate. This is best reflected in the assumptions of evolution, the big bang theory or abiogenesis. These are all theories themselves based on some selected evidence and facts that are processed based on human limited knowledge and bias, and produce wrong theories.

The statement reads:

No matter how well you analyze the sand in the desert and no matter how precisely you count the grains of sand in the desert, it will still be a desert.

Here we come to a better variant.

In order for someone to believe that we ate, that someone can witness how we prepare food and how we eat. However, there is no evidence here. The man attended our meal through subjective experience and he does not believe based on evidence but personal experience that we ate.

However, even this is not enough because the observer does not have the experience of the taste of the food, he did not eat it. To have the full experience he must eat.

What is the conclusion here?

Looking for evidence does not solve the problem of ignorance. To believe in the theories of scientists is to believe in the minds of other people. Many people claim that there is evidence for some theories, but this is not true. Those people do not have a conscious knowledge of the theories of scientists, nor do they have knowledge or understanding of these evidences (as with many scientists). These people only believe in the theories of scientists and believe in "evidence" that they have not assimilated experientially.

What am I explaining here?

Looking for evidence is ignorance and lack of experience, and therefore the belief that the truth can be reached through circumstantial evidence, which is a denial of one's own life and experience. It is the same as when a person believes that with the help of a calculator he will find the truth contained in Creation.

You can claim something based on experience and not evidence.

To say that subjective experience is unreliable is insecurity. In reality, there is no better and more reliable proof.

Do you need someone to prove and explain to you how you live, what you think, what you do and what you experience?

Conclusion: people look for proof when they do not value their life and their experiences and when they do not realize that they are capable of doing everything on their own.

Simply put: Can "evidence" or looking for evidence convince you that you haven't ate?

FAITH IN EVIDENCE

The situation is very simple.

God created the Cosmos and the laws by which the Universe exists.

Atheists try to call these laws evolution.

The modern theory of evolution presented to us by scientists is not correct.

It is only imagination of the mind based on limited evidence and facts.

The theory of evolution is a belief system, because belief is really necessary for facts and evidence that are circumstantial and variable in nature.

Conclusion:

Much more faith is required in the theory of evolution than in God.

You can experience God experientially, but not the invented theory of evolution.

WHAT IS EVOLUTION AND WHAT IS CREATIONISM?

Evolution has nothing to do with creationism except for two things.

If it claims to know the origin of creation (which it certainly will never know) and if it claims the development of life from a single cell (which is pure nonsense).

So the whole theory of evolution (fictional and real) has nothing to do with creationism.

Creationism is valid because God is the Creator of everything. Changes in Creation are not a problem of creationism but of evolution.

However, keep in mind that evolution deals with the past, so many theories will be wrong and are mere belief systems.

Why?

Statements without subjective experience are not certain knowledge. It can never be proven or confirmed.

That is why you can recognize a man who does not know by the fact that he is looking for evidence, not subjective confirmation.

EVOLUTION AGAINST THE THEORY OF EVOLUTION

The fact is that the word evolution means positive progress. The word evolution has its place and meaning.

One of the main meanings is the evolution of consciousness. With the evolution of consciousness comes the evolution of society, the evolution of knowledge, the progress of technology, science, etc...

To say that evolution exists is true, but to say that the modern scientific theory of evolution is true is an outright lie.

This is very easy to explain.

A man may kill for love, but the murder will not be love but murder.

There is an evolution of something, but the theory of evolution (today) does not exist and has never happened because the evidence is not reliable.

Conclusion:

The only evolution that certainly exists is the evolution of consciousness. God created the world so that every soul could attain perfect consciousness. If scientists knew this, then they would come to better conclusions.

Therefore, all species created by God have a task for a certain development of soul consciousness. Accordingly, many things evolve in the Cosmos.

The materialistic theory of evolution is pure mind numbing and falsification of the past because spiritual laws follow God, matter follows spiritual laws, so material changes are the least important and impossible to prove for the past.

SIMPLE MATH

When we go out into the world and see dinosaurs and live with them, it is direct experience and knowledge. It may not be complete but it is real.

On the other hand, a billion fossils found do not prove a single dinosaur, because any experiential processing of the evidence is a fiction of the mind based on the belief in circumstantial evidence, method and a limited mind.

WHICH IS BETTER?

If you take a little time and pay attention, you will see that there are countless evidences of God, either through perfect logic, or through perfect love, or through a series of paradoxes of creation that no scientist will ever explain.

Therefore, ignorance and failure to recognize that evidence are not arguments.

If the world claims that there is no proof of God, it only means that the whole world is in the dark. However, I argue that it is not so. Many people know God, but there are too many who have abandoned the Self and knowledge because of belief in evidence.

So what is better, to know the Self or to explore the Cosmos?

RELIGION AND FAITH

BAD DEFINITION OF FAITH (or belief, it's the same for me)
If I ate and you believe that I ate, how is that ignorance or untruth?

Or, to put it more simply, doesn't this mean that when children go to school to be educated, their education is based on a belief in something they don't know?

Double standard.

Absurd.

FAITH IN GOD IS PRIMARY KNOWLEDGE
Many philosophers argue that subjective experience is uncertain and that evidence is necessary.

This is a fallacy and I can easily prove it.

Subjective experience is also necessary for the validation of evidence. This means that faith in evidence is weaker than faith in experience because you also have to deal with circumstantial evidence through the limited mind.

As you can see, faith in God through experience is the safest, then everything else.

SPIRITUAL TEACHINGS
Each religion is a special spiritual path and a special teaching with the same goal.

Religion is not just belief in God. Religion is both knowledge and experience about God and about the spiritual path. Everything depends on the level of consciousness of a person and on the spiritual experiences that person has had.

FUN SPIRITUALITY

To classify religion and any spiritual teaching only as faith is a wrong assumption.

FAITH AND KNOWLEDGE

There is a contemporary statement that says:
– I don't want to believe, I want to know.
We can debunk this fallacy with a simple sentence:
– I know experientially that God exists, but I do not believe that God exists.
What is the conclusion?
Note:
The sentence is not fixed. We can also say "I ate but I don't believe I ate", or "I know the Earth is round but I don't believe the Earth is round"...

TRANSIENT RELIGION

Atheism is considered a passing belief.
What does that mean?
A transitory religion arose in the mind, as an assumption, belief, or doubt. More precisely, it is a false religion without real knowledge or experience. People very quickly abandon such beliefs because falsehood does not bring fulfillment.
Why do people, say, worship Islam, Buddhism or Christianity?
Those religions rest on the magnificent works, truths and love of Allah, Buddha and Jesus.
Claiming that religion is not spirituality is the same as claiming that the sun will not shine on a religious person. However, it is only when that man rises to the Sun that we realize that the Sun is shining on that man.
Trying to convince people that religion is not spirituality is creating a new temporary religion.

Why transient?

People are not stupid. The fact that you see deluded people around you is a current condition, because people have to learn and grow spiritually through experiences. Delusion is never a final or final state. To say that religion is not an inner spiritual path is a fallacy.

That is why the works of the Avatar and the Messiah will shine forever.

HOW TO FIND GOD?

Knowledge is not science. Knowledge is not philosophy. Knowledge is not atheism.

Knowledge is God.

A compass always points north.

What does that mean?

Our heart is a compass. The mind is not.

God is knowledge and love. Mind is delusion and slavery.

If this is true, then what is the problem?

The problem is the fact that when a man begins to follow his heart, people ridicule and trample on that man. The trouble is that you don't know and you want to know, and ignorance shakes you because you care about the opinions and actions of the ignorant (out of ignorance complex).

Therefore, not finding God is always a problem of faith and nothing else.

PHILOSOPHICAL ERRORS

CONSCIOUSNESS AND THE EGOCENTRIC MIND

Consciousness is something we all have.

By expanding our consciousness we gain the power of love, compassion, perception and morality.

Therefore, our actions mostly depend on the level of our consciousness.

The beginning of our actions can be found in the mind and in the thoughts in the mind. However, we determine with our consciousness which idea we will realize and what we will believe.

Therefore, perfect consciousness contains perfect action.

God possesses perfect consciousness and that is why God, whether in the form of Creator or Sustainer or in the form of man, has perfect action.

So many people glorify the mind and intelligence which are the properties of the ego and the ego will never reach the truth and God. It is the same for you as if you had a calculator and if you believed that with the help of the digitron you would realize God. And whatever experience you have you want your digitron to calculate your experience. In this way, a person closes his eyes to the facts and relies on the delusional calculations of the digitron.

So, where does the main obstacle in philosophy lie?

It is hidden in the fact that many philosophers want to determine God and creation in the mind, which is impossible. The mind is used for thinking. Consciousness is built on experience. A man who cannot get out of the construction of the mind will never know the truth. And the mind wants to explain everything and understand everything.

When you go out into the street and see the Sun, you have an experience and no one has to explain anything to you. You experience everything directly. If someone needs to explain such an experience to you, you are in ignorance and inexperience.

If someone explains something to you through experiential knowledge, if you believe it, you will have knowledge but not experience. Again, you will have to gain experience based on that knowledge, otherwise you will be just a believer without experiential knowledge.

Many philosophers are believers without experiential knowledge. Some believe in falsehood, some believe in some true things.

Belief in a perfect Creator God is the only correct initial faith. Everything else is eternal wandering through the rainforest.

So a hypothetical eternal hell exists. It is eternal disbelief in God (which fortunately cannot be eternal).

THE WATCHMAKER ANALOGY

The very paradox of mother and child is proof of God the Creator.

What does that mean?

There is an analogy that every watch has a designer who made that watch. This indicates that everything in the world has a Creator – a Designer.

It is said that the watchmaker's analogy is not correct because it cannot be proof that the world has an intelligent creator.

However, doubting such a statement does not prove that the watchmaker's analogy is incorrect. Doubt and conjecture have never been proof of anything. Likewise, doubting the watchmaker's analogy does not prove that the analogy is incorrect.

So if I eat food to live, that doesn't mean everyone has to eat food to live?

If every child has a mother, doesn't that mean every mother has a mother?

If a watch has its own designer, that doesn't mean the designer is a product of God the Creator?

The watchmaker analogy has not been proven wrong because there is no evidence to disprove the analogy. And that proof does not exist because the analogy is correct.

God is the Creator. Every man can know God. God is also a proof that proves himself. I don't see what's unclear there?

In order to create the first child in creation, God created a mother capable of giving birth and created man to provide the material necessary for fertilization. It is the law that God created for us.

This is proof that God is so powerful that he created a perfect world in an instant where souls can live forever if they want to.

Therefore, the beginning is the same as the end of creation. There is no difference.

Nothing evolves in the world except our consciousness.

With the evolution of consciousness we find God. We become aware of God. In the end, we get to know who we are.

THE BEGINNING OF LOGIC

All of Creation and all of your life are evidence of God.

Seeking evidence of God from others is actually a deception that knows no evidence.

Atheism is a delusion of the mind.

How do I know that?

Perfect logic recognizes a perfect Creator, a perfect Creation and a perfect meaning–goal.

Any other logic is human ignorance and deception.

BURDEN OF PROOF

There is no burden of proof. If someone asks for proof from other people, that person claims that it is possible and obligatory which is only an assumption that does not affect the truth.

In that case, the burden of proof is borne by the person requesting the proof. That person must make the request for evidence valid otherwise he/she has no right to set conditions.

There are many things in life that are impossible to prove except through subjective experience.

Therefore, many philosophical expressions (I believe atheistic) such as atheism, burden of proof, ad hominem, strawman fallacy, logical fallacy, begging the question and many others are pure fallacies because they do not have truth (knowledge) as a starting point, but only opinion, where it is absurd to set rules and definitions for such situations when you know nothing and only assume.

If is not clear to someone, the one setting the conditions has no knowledge, so any rule he claims someone needs to prove to him has no validity in many cases. Therefore, each of these definitions of waste.

RULE OF EVIDENCE

Belief in the rule of evidence is one of the biggest misconceptions of today.

This rule is confirmed every day as uncertain and yet people still believe in this rule.

That's what marketing does, not reason. Believing in the served delusion without critical thinking and without accepting what is happening in reality.

FRAUDULENCE OF FACTS AND EVIDENCE

The only immutable fact is that facts are changeable and the only real evidence is that the evidences are states that do not yield certain knowledge and truth.

The theory of facts and evidence falls apart even more easily when we realize that a biased, limited and ignorant mind must process them.

So what are we left with?

We are left with a personal, conscious experience that must be assimilated and accepted.

What's the best thing about it?

You have no false intermediary in the form of facts and evidence.

Example:

This is proof that the theory of evolution may have facts and evidence, but no knowledge and truth, because there is no personal experience or knowledge.

Simply put, the theory of evolution is a belief based on belief in limited facts and evidence. It is a double belief, and it is already a superstition.

The lesson is:

Believe in yourself, God, your life and your experience.

We have just proved that knowledge also requires faith. Do not be ashamed of your faith even if you have no knowledge, because faith is knowledge in the future. Faith is the precursor of knowledge and then became knowledge.

FALLACY

There are many definitions of different logical fallacies in philosophy.

What many philosophers do not yet understand is the fact that an ignorant person cannot determine what a logical fallacy is.

I can easily explain this on the example of an atheist.

Many people have come to know God. A man who has realized God has the right to claim that atheism, which claims that God does not exist and that no one has proven God, is a logical fallacy.

An atheist who has no knowledge of God has no right to claim that no one has known God based on the delusion that one needs to prove the existence of God on the material plane.

If you were to ask for the existence of someone's love or your thoughts to be materially proven, it would be a logical fallacy, wouldn't it?

This is proof that atheism is a proven logical fallacy.

Therefore, any claim that God does not exist and that no one has proven God is false and a logical fallacy.

PHILOSOPHY AS IGNORANCE

Philosophy will never gain true knowledge until spiritual teachings are conducted on a subjective experiential level.

This is also the reason why philosophy has never found the truth, but deals with wandering in the mind and looking for holes in assertions and statements that have no support in real life.

This is the reason why metaphysics has failed, and therefore the whole of philosophy. Rejecting the spiritual and acknowledging the mental and material is self–limitation. It is the rejection of self and life and the acceptance of mind, thought and matter. You can come up with anything in your mind, but it all remains in the limited mind as a thought without experiential knowledge, which does not represent a general truth but only a thought.

Philosophy must come out of the mind.

The whole philosophy so far is based on the fantasy "as someone nicely and cleverly said it".

However, there is no real truth in philosophy. In some parts of philosophy, the goal is determined, but the method and direction are not. This is only found in religions and spiritual teachings.

It is because of the focus on the mind. Metaphysicians quite naively came to the conclusion that the primary cause cannot be known, which is a wrong assumption.

From that error comes all the ignorance of philosophy.

God as the primary cause, sustainer, means and goal is attainable, but cannot be grasped by the mind.

The mind is a creation and the mind is limited and mortal.

Soul and consciousness are not.

Conclusion:

The fallacy of philosophy is reflected in the fact that many want to separate knowledge from God, which is absurd because God is knowledge, truth and freedom. It's like trying to separate a child from its mother's womb.

Knowledge about God is basic knowledge on the basis of which you get conclusive knowledge (it is not wandering and wrong).

LET'S BE RATIONAL

Many people accuse me of using the words "evidence" or "fact" lightly because they have no experiential knowledge of it and believe that it is not objective evidence. However, it is only man's forgetfulness to recognize wondrous truths in a simple way.

Here's a simple one:

The fact that man can live without an arm or a leg is proof that we are not a body but a God-soul who uses the body to experience life on planet Earth and reach truth, knowledge and superconsciousness.

Someone will say that it is not evidence, but they will not be right because they just do not recognize evidence from ignorance, and that ignorance is caused by belief in objective evidence.

But what is objective evidence? These are established misconceptions about creation. And creation is a consequence. When looking at the effects, the cause remains unrecognizable. And the cause is literally everything and every person is capable of knowing God. It is the most wonderful law and gift from God to us.

ATHEISM AS DOUBT AND IGNORANCE

MY WORK

The purpose of my work is to discover what people think and do with the help of certain experiences. Based on that, I present my conclusions in my texts.

When people experience the truth I'm talking about, those people spread that truth further as they wish.

World consciousness is changing and no one can stop it.

The second task I have set myself is to challenge atheistic ignorance. When confronted with knowledge of God and Self and valid claims, the atheist must accept his own ignorance and delusion.

In this way, the consciousness of atheists also changes. No one can stop that.

Atheism is an ignorant belief that has no purpose or hope.

What do I want to explain?

The knowledge of God will spread throughout the world. Atheists, as always, will have to put up with it.

ATHEISM IS NOT A LACK OF FAITH IN GOD

If atheism were a lack of belief in God, then the word atheism would not exist.

It's the same as if someone didn't ski, then they should be called a non-skier.

Atheism means the belief that God does not exist. That is an assertion and as far as we can see proven ignorance.

EVIDENCE OR PROOF OF GOD

There are indirect and direct evidences in the Serbian language.

Circumstantial evidence should lead you to the only real conclusion – the truth.

Using logic, the only correct true conclusion would be "evidence" in English in my understanding. Also, the English have another expression, which is "proof". Proof should be true confirmation on the physical plane.

Now, many people, especially atheists, like to look for "evidence" of God (because they have found that looking for proof is ridiculous and incorrect.

However, looking for a final true conclusion based on logic is also not reliable because such a thing requires a perfect beginning and a perfect logic and a perfect conclusion. Few people have that. More precisely, the search for "evidence" (truth) and proof is carried out improperly in most cases, so any person can deny the real truth. This means that you consider evidence that is evidence to be no evidence at all.

When an atheist asks for proof of God, it is ridiculous because how can what is created prove the Creator?

That's why atheists are now looking for "evidence".

Of course, that is also a fallacy.

The proof of God, and therefore the "evidence" is Creation or God himself.

Both the evidence and the proof of God is the immediate personal experience of God.

Therefore, evidence and proof for God exist, but people are not able to understand that it is only a direct knowledge and revelation of God and nothing else.

Of course, the evidence also include conversations with God and certain spiritual experiences, same as world and life but all of these have no points of contact with the physical world, nor with intelligence.

The lesson is:

Looking for proof of God is a straw man fallacy if one does not realize that the only proof is God himself and the experience of God. In this way, the request to seek proof through Creation is incorrect, it leads to error.

Therefore, no proof of God is sought, but rather knowledge and a way to know God.

DEAF–MUMBLED GOD

The most terrifying thing in the Cosmos is the deaf and dumb God.

Atheists have created such a God in their minds.

It is a God who does not listen to our prayers and does not answer them.

That is the only God created by atheists. Such a God is not real.

Nevertheless, the real God sees, hears and helps, primarily to people who want to see, hear and ask for help.

BAD FAITH

By believing that you are doing the right thing because you believe the opposite of the beliefs of those you hate, you are doing yourself harm and being dependent on those people.

Therefore, the statement that some people believe wrongly so you must do the opposite is probably also wrongly believing.

I see no benefit from such behavior.

If anyone doesn't understand what I'm trying to say: With this kind of thinking and belief, bad believers are bound to affect you negatively, even when you believe you're righteous.

DEMAND OF ATHEISTS FOR EVIDENCE OF GOD

Atheist:

– All claims must be supported by evidence and the evidence must be objectively verifiable, otherwise it is not evidence.

Me:

– Ok. Give me evidence for your claim.

Atheist:

– What claim?

Asking people for evidence of God is a claim for which the seekers have no evidence at all to be the rule.

That is why no atheist has discovered God.

ATHEISTIC "CRITICAL THINKING"

Have you noticed that atheists only have questions and not answers?

They even answer a question with a question.

Why?

This is because making up answers is recognizable.

However, inventing incorrect questions requires impossible answers that no one can answer.

That's why atheists like to believe that endlessly inventing questions without finding answers is critical thinking.

ATHEISM IS FALSE LOGIC

If an atheist thought about the concept of God, he would never ask such an arbitrary and illogical question.

To prove the Creator by creation?

Imagine digging a hole without anyone knowing.

The stranger walks past the holes. The hole is evidence that you dug it, but the stranger doesn't know that and doesn't want to accept the claim.

Who is responsible?

The one who looks at the evidence and does not admit the evidence because he thinks that he should not admit the evidence is responsible.

All creation is evidence of God. And what is an atheist looking for? "Give me evidence of God".

Arbitrary, wrong request. You cannot ask others to do what you have to do. God is a personal achievement, just like love and experience.

Atheism is proven ignorance and flawed logic. Fallacy of ignorance.

ATHEISTIC DOUBT

Atheism is endless questioning and doubting every answer.

What does that mean?

When you present knowledge, truth, fact and experience to an atheist, the atheist does not understand it because he does not possess any of it.

More precisely, an atheist cannot recognize truth, knowledge, or even any evidence, because an atheist has no knowledge and experience of it. That's why for him every evidence and every truth is a doubt.

Based on misunderstanding, ignorance and doubt, the atheist asks new questions, which when you answer him, the atheist doubts again and admits neither truth nor evidence, but only sees a claim that you need to prove to him.

However, you cannot prove anything to an ignorant person because an ignorant person does not know, and an ignorant person only doubts.

So atheism is endless doubt and asking the wrong questions. The proof is that an atheist never gives knowledge or answers in a discussion, but only doubts and asks questions (exactly where everything is explained and already answered).

ATHEISM AS IGNORANCE HAS NO DEBATE

Atheist:

– I am not claiming anything except that there is no proof of God and that God must be proven the way I want. I also claim that no one has known God and I claim that the non-existence of God cannot be proven.

I also argue that God must be proven in a scientific fictional way which in reality is not scientific but atheistic infidel. I claim that my assumptions, questions and requests are not incorrect and based on the imagination of the mind.

I claim much more. I claim that God does not exist and I do not believe in God, which means that I do not claim anything and I do not believe in anything.

Therefore, any intelligent person can understand:

Atheism does not assert anything by asking questions and demands and this proves that everyone must adapt to the mental demands of atheists because that is what we want and that is "right".

Atheists certainly don't have to prove anything to anyone while everyone else has to behave according to the ignorant fabrication of atheism(?).

Atheist rules apply to everyone but atheists(?).

Conclusion:

An atheist knows nothing and believes in nothing. It is the basis for asking the right questions, demands and claims?

Real logic!

A simple solution:

–For anything an atheist asks you for proof/evidence, you ask him for evidence that the claims hidden in his request or question are correct. You will see that no atheist will ever have a valid answer and will be defeated in debate with his weapons.

Let's say, if an atheist asks you for evidence of God, you have the right to ask him what the evidence is that indicates that you are responsible for giving him evidence of God and how he has proof that there must be material proof of God. And of course, how is he sure that the world is no longer evidence of God, because the God who created the world logically means that everything created IS evidence of God.

WHY ATHEISTS DO NOT KNOW GOD?
Student:
–Teacher, why don't atheists know you?
Teacher:
– I live here outside evil and ignorance, on the seventh floor. You went out of your way to come here to find me. Atheists are just waiting on the first floor where I don't reveal myself for someone to bring them a reward.

If you want to know me, you have to find me. That's the only fair way.
You know what they do?
They are looking for proof.
Even when I give them proof that I exist, they still don't know Me, so they don't even recognize the proof.

ATHEISM IS IGNORANCE
Atheist:
– God is an imaginary friend. – said the atheist with an imaginary experience and proof.
Why would an atheist claim that God is an imaginary friend?
Conclusion:
Atheism is an entire logical fallacy.
Atheist:
–Give me proof of God.
The assumption that man is more powerful than God.

Conclusion:
Atheism is all a logical fallacy, but in this case it's also impertinence.
Atheist:
–Which God is real?
The assumption that there are many Gods based on a misinterpretation of spiritual teachings and religions. One is in the multitude and the multitude is one.
Conclusion:
Atheism is all a logical fallacy.
Atheist:
– We don't have proof of God, but God killed many people.
Conclusion:
Atheism is all a logical fallacy.
Atheist:
– Creation is not proof of God. Why not? Creation and life are direct signatures of God.
Conclusion:
Atheism is all a logical fallacy.
Atheist:
– I am not claiming anything. – said the atheist, claiming that he does not claim anything.
Conclusion:
Atheism is all a logical fallacy.
Atheist:
– We are food for worms. – said the atheist who does not know who he is and does not know where he comes from or where he is going.
Conclusion:
Atheism is all a logical fallacy.
Atheist:
–Atheism is not a belief. – said an atheist who believes that atheism is not a belief.
Conclusion:

Atheism is a false belief.
General conclusion:
—Atheism is total ignorance because it is based on a false assumption:
Denying and doubting God who is knowledge and truth: the false assumption that God does not exist and that someone is obliged to give us proof.

HOW?

5000 years ago they asked an atheist why he didn't believe in God.
The atheist replied:
— Because no one has proven God.
But, faith in evidence is proven uncertain belief. — people told him.
Even after 5000 years an atheist claims the same.
It's not the same though. These are the new atheists. The old ones are no longer atheists.
So how do you get out of atheism?
Very simple.
Stop asking the wrong questions and ask the right question.
Which is the correct question?
The correct question is:
— How to know God?
There is already an easy answer. You only need to read any passage from any religious scriptures, even if there are 5000 of them, and you will get the way and the path, which you only need to follow.
There you go.

EXIT FROM IGNORANCE

If you look at the entire history, you will recognize the fact that every atheist has a lifelong lack of basic knowledge about himself.

Getting out of atheism is getting out of the vicious cycle of doubt and ignorance.

ATHEISM AND JESUS

Atheist:

– God does not exist because there is no evidence of God (except the entire Universe). Jesus did not exist because there is no evidence that he existed (except that there is).

Easy question:

–Find five facts that prove the total stupidity of these statements.

Difficult (impossible) question:

–Find only one valid argument in these statements.

More natural:

– What no one has ever proven in the entire history is the knowledge of atheism. Atheistic knowledge does not exist, and it has been proven.

SOURCE

The atheist bathes in the river and asks:

Where does this river come from?

Me:

– From the source.

Atheist:

– I don't see any source. Prove to me that the source exists.

Me:

– You have to go to the source yourself to see for yourself.

Atheist:

– You have no proof, so the source does not exist.

ATHEISTIC "CRITICAL THINKING" HAS NO KNOWLEDGE

Critical thinking is when you examine things and get to the truth.

Atheists only doubt, ask questions, believe, assume, but never give knowledge and truth.

So, atheism is not critical thinking at all, but ignorance that requires others to give it knowledge.

So pay attention to atheist posts and comments.

All the questions and inventing definitions of how someone else should know something and give it to us.

PREJUDICES OF ATHEISM

The idea of atheism that science has rationality because it seeks evidence that is never necessarily true and that spirituality and God have no evidence as subjective experience is a logical fallacy that refuses to be corrected.

How long will philosophy adapt to one-sided incorrect rules and logical fallacies?

Creationist:
– Women love sex.
Evolutionist:
– How do you know?
Creationist:
– I experienced it.
Evolutionist:
– So you have no proof. You don't know.
Evolutionist:
– Women love sex.
Creationist:
– How do you know?
Evolutionist:

– I read books and examine the evidence.

Creationist:

–Books and evidence cannot give you experiential knowledge.

This is proof that human experience is rational and real, while evolutionism is a reliance on processing matter and a lack of experiential knowledge.

ATHEISM HAS NO FAITH IN SELF AND EXPERIENCE

There are thousands of religions in the world. Each of these religions worships the form of God, the name and attributes of God. That's why every religion has knowledge and a path.

Only atheism never has knowledge. Opting for doubt without any logic or premise, atheism condemned itself to eternal ignorance and doubt.

That's why atheism is always, but always, a delusion based on ignorance. It cannot be otherwise.

Logical, right? How can ignorance and doubt produce knowledge? Not at all.

You have to believe, do something and know God and the truth.

SPIRITUAL EGO

A SEA OF MISUNDERSTANDING

Contemporary spirituality is experiencing complete banalization.

The differences between good and evil, truth and untruth, correctness and incorrectness, knowledge and ignorance are erased.

Everything is thrown into the same basket.

People try to push God out of spirituality as well. People want to replace God with Creation and God's attributes. By perfecting the attributes we attain God. Yet God is a living, omnipotent, impersonal entity. God is not an attribute. More precisely, God assigned perfect attributes to himself (he could not do otherwise) as the perfect ruler of the Universe. In that way, the universe is just and safe, perfect.

Avoiding God is the result of man's inner injuries.

So what's good here?

In the sea of ignorance, some truth is found.

Still, even that is much better than when the truth is forbidden.

While the transformation continues, ignorance reigns.

Good luck!

BE A WISE SNAKE THAT DOES NOT BITE

When you hide the truth from other people, you judge those people.

How and why?

A man who does not know the truth lives in ignorance.

Man does evil deeds out of ignorance.

A person who does wrong and evil deeds gets suffering and misfortune.

This reminds me of the story of the snake that the Guru told not to bite. After some time, when he saw snake beaten, the snake told him that she not bite and that people mistreat her.

Guru said: – I told you not to bite, not to not hiss.

In relation to our topic: you don't need to punish people, but it is your duty to tell the truth and spread knowledge. And the truth is always unpleasant and bitter for those who do not live it.

The lesson is:

As much as your spiritual knowledge, so are your good deeds, and so is your karma.

Therefore, never confuse spiritual knowledge with worldly knowledge. Science is responsible for secular knowledge.

Spiritual knowledge knows God, love, morality and right action.

KNOWLEDGE AND OPINION

Once knowledge was valued, today opinion is valued.

What does that mean?

One of the negative aspects of modern spirituality is that hardly anyone knows what spirituality is.

Magnificent truths are described in religions. The modern spiritualist proclaims religion as dogma while at the same time believing in lion portals and fifth dimensions.

What is this about?

A spiritual charlatan is a man who does not understand that spirituality is the pursuit of God, that God is a perfectly attainable entity, and that God is perfectly merciful and just.

Natural learning: There is nothing worse than an ignorant person setting the rules for you in spirituality.

That is why modern spirituality is in many ways ridiculous (if it can be called spirituality at all).

The lesson is:

If you don't know ask the one who knows and follow him.

It's not a shame.

It's a shame when you don't know, but you set the rules and pretend you do.

More precisely, the rule that you should respect everyone's opinion was created to avoid conflicts, and not to respect your own and other people's ignorance and wrong thinking and actions through false sanctity.

It is pure tyranny of the human mind and has nothing to do with spirituality.

DOGMA TOWARDS ONESELF

Should we ditch all textbooks and let children learn everything on their own from scratch?

There is a statement that says:

– Some have bad luck and some have a spiritual teacher. You can't have both.

A spiritual master is the same as a billionaire in the physical world. If he likes you, he gives you everything you need.

At this point I have two questions:

1. Is truth a dogma and does that mean that a teaching that leads to a goal is a dogma?

2. Is being burdened with the right that you can have the wrong opinion and that you can go the wrong way in reality a dogma towards yourself?

PICTURE

If the Universe is the image, God is the content (of course, the analogy is not perfect, but it makes the point).

Because of access to content, there are many religions and spiritual teachings.

This means that many religions are correct in their own way.

Bigotry towards any religion due to misunderstanding of scriptures could not be called spirituality, could it?

VISION OF GOD

I often feel the need to emphasize that from a worldly point of view God is not energy.

Many people say that God is energy without any good explanation.

God created energy, vibration and frequency. Then people say that the soul is energy that vibrates at a certain high frequency.

We can solve this misconception with the following statement:

– Man is God, but God is not man.

Explain this truth in any practical way.

SPIRITUAL EDUCATION

Religious intolerance is ignorance.

What does that mean?

Religion is the way to God. Contemporary spirituality should be a path to God otherwise it is not true spirituality.

I can prove it very easily.

In religions there are basic universal truths. Based on those truths, many people have attained God.

Any man who wanted to change the meaning and purpose of Creation had to face his own delusion and declare his own failure.

Therefore, there are always many more people who would rather wander after their own desires and delusions than seek for God.

That's why most people don't like religion. Even many members of religions who were born there hate their own religion.

What happened in the not so distant past?

A philosophy was created.

What is characteristic of many philosophers?

It is characteristic that they worship the mind, therefore they also worship intelligence and logic. Throughout time philosophers have given many intelligent sayings but no philosopher has found God. The reason is that due to the worship of the mind, the knowledge of God was abandoned, so religions and God were thrown out of philosophy. And what can philosophy know and a man who does not know who he is, what God is and where he is going?

Today's modern spirituality tries to explain to us that each of us has a special relationship with God, which is very good because it is true. However, in the very next moment, modern clergymen show that they do not know what spirituality is and do not know how to build a relationship with God.

This means that modern spiritualists are trying to return to the level of caveman consciousness. Rejecting the knowledge of God and the way to God is exactly that.

Imagine a contemporary cleric denigrating the work of a Jesus or Buddha or almighty Allah? So what can that man know and what kind of enlightenment can that man have?

Conclusion:

Religions will not be extinguished for the simple reason that there are many members of religions and because it is ridiculous for a person to think that he will destroy God and the truth with desire and marketing, and still believe that in this way he will save himself and humanity.

Here I will point out another funny thing. Modern clergy claim to have their own relationship with God that religious people don't?

The statement that spirituality is faith in one's own experience and that religion is faith in someone else's experience is precisely a fallacy.

By believing in someone else's true experience, you gain your own experience. A modern clergyman who has no experience of God has a lack of experience.

So lack of experience is not experience, and not being aware of God is not your conscious relationship with God even though the relationship exists.

JUDGMENT OR COMMON SENSE?

Discerning good and evil is a very high spiritual discipline.

Many spiritualists today mistakenly call this discipline a judging.

Judging is when you punish someone. When you evaluate, for example, a certain behavior, it is not a judgment but a teaching of common sense.

For example, if I say that smoking is very harmful, I have not condemned anyone, but stated the truth and manifested knowledge. To say that I judge smokers for this statement is an exaggeration.

Why is this important?

False kindness counts as hidden violence.

When you try to reject evil and violence from yourself and someone does not allow you to discover correct behavior under the explanation that everyone has the right to think and do what they want and that it is none of your business, such a person does violence to society and prevents the victory over ignorance.

So, if you don't know the difference between good and evil, how will you progress spiritually and how will you gain knowledge and truth?

Where is the morality?

The lesson is:

Do not fall for false holiness and false goodness because you will suffer great damage on the inner plane.

FOOD FOR PHILOSOPHERS

LYING?
Shouldn't we really tell a liar that he's a liar because we're going to hurt his feelings?

Do you really believe that a liar does not hurt anyone when he lies?

What does it even mean when you defend a liar?

UNIVERSE AS EVIDENCE
"The universe is evidence of itself, not an evidence of God".

This is a logical fallacy based on ignorance.

Ignorance does not determine what knowledge or evidence is.

EVIDENCE OF GOD
Atheist:

– There is no evidence of God.

Me:

–Except for all of life and all of Creation which is of course a small amount of evidence for an atheist.

WHEN WILL WE GET FREE OF IGNORANCE AND TRICKS?
Let's start from the fact that Socrates, by declaring that he knows nothing, freed himself from the responsibility of knowledge and in this way gave the Sufis the task of proving what they claim to know.

That's what atheists do today.

Atheists constantly claim that they do not know and constantly look for other people's knowledge, but they do not have their own.

However, there is a big difference here.

Socrates displayed knowledge.

The position of atheism is very dishonest. They ask others to do everything for them. Socrates not only did not ask but gave his life for the truth, that is, for what he KNEW!

And what did Socrates know?

He knew God and truth and knowledge. The statement that he knew nothing was about atheism. That only God knows and man as an ego does not know.

Atheism is the worship of mind and ego, and therefore the cultivation of ignorance. Socrates knew this.

FOOD FOR THE MIND

HE WHO HAS NOTHING to believe in is in obvious ignorance.

ATHEISM IS SELF–PERCEIVED ignorance, which the atheist, if he does not notice, certainly ignores. There is no logic in either case.

WHY DOES SCIENCE HAVE no real knowledge?

Because it has no knowledge of God, consciousness, love, character, morality, truth, happiness, compassion, faith and freedom.

God with his attributes is the only true and truly necessary knowledge.

Scientific knowledge is similar to today's idea of the matrix. Determining the rules and conditions of delusion.

FUN SPIRITUALITY

FACT:
−Rationality finds God. This is proof that science is irrational with its rules and methods and does not have the knowledge necessary for man.

IF DIRECT PERSONAL experience counts as evidence then why do those who do not know define knowledge?

THE PARADOX OF MOTHER and child is one of the proofs of God the Creator.

And not only that.

This is proof that considerations of the origin and age of the Universe do not make any sense.

SOMETIMES IT HAPPENS that a married couple gets divorced and then one spouse says:

− I loved my partner but I don't love him anymore.

You see, it's not proof that your partner doesn't exist or that relationship with your partner didn't work. It is proof that you have betrayed your partner.

SCIENCE IS GUESSWORK.

HOW CAN SOMETHING THAT a man abandoned with death be a reality?

IGNORANCE OF GOD IS evidence of real ignorance.

YOU HAVE TO BELIEVE the "evidence" anyway. That's a fact.

HE WHO THINKS IS HE who does not know.

HOW DO YOU DISTINGUISH between the inner and the outer world?

NOT BELIEVING IS NOT knowing.

IF YOU ALREADY HAVE so much faith in the evidence, why don't you notice the million pieces of evidence that prove the rule of evidence is insecure?

FACT:
    – Nothing in the world and in life happens without God's approval.

SCIENCE IS JUST A BIGGER superstition than faith in an imperfect God.

IT IS A VERY STRANGE destruction through unbelief in God that insists on eternal ignorance and despair.

WE FIGHT FOR THE POSITIVE TRANSFORMATION OF CHRISTIANITY

JESUS' WORK AND TEACHING ARE PERFECT

I am very happy about the fact that social networks have progressed so that we can all talk about religious teachings from home, from the armchair, which gives us a quick transfer of information and opinions.

History has shown us that not understanding the scriptures and not following the teachings can even lead to wars.

Here I want to think about one fact that has brought a lot of intolerance towards Christianity.

It is the idea of one worldly life and eternal hell.

From my point of view, and therefore from the point of view of a perfect God, these two statements of Jesus have been misunderstood and imposed on believers.

When Jesus said that there is only one life, it did not mean one worldly life because the soul must be born again until it has paid off its debts and attained perfection. Jesus thought of birth as the creation of the soul and death as the death of the ego, the return to God.

In this way, the belief that God is unjust was created because we all witness the different destinies and life conditions of each person. Our birth and our current life is a consequence of actions from previous lives.

Jesus spoke of one life because he knew that life.

This idea continued with the idea of eternal hell, which if you think about it only makes hypothetical sense. It is the idea that Jesus warned that continually doing wrong deeds leaves one in hell with righteous consequences. Therefore, every soul is taken out of "hell" by doing only good deeds. The conclusion that one goes to eternal hell after death is a fallacy and a misinterpretation of the perfect Jesus and teachings.

Here is also added the belief that one will avoid the consequences of actions by confessing or repenting, and if we just look, Jesus himself had to be born to burn the sins of humanity on the cross, which proves the law of creation that what you do will definitely come back to you because Jesus suffering on the cross shows that even God respects that law and sacrificed himself for humanity.

However, Christianity, like any other religion, is perfect, and the great privilege of the Christian religion is the perfect example of the messiah, Jesus Christ, who is not only there to teach, but also to set an example and deliver and give freedom. So maybe even the most grateful religion.

Why did I write this text?

I believe that the time is ripe for us to know the work of Jesus in the right light and to understand the love and perfection of Jesus, God and Christian teaching. The people who lived at the time of Jesus were largely tragedians so they made the message of Jesus somewhat tragic. True, but tragic because of a wrong view of God and the work of Jesus.

What do you think? Is it possible after so much time, not to change, but to correctly understand, perfect and transmit Jesus' teaching?

Do you also believe that there is no other way then perfect God, love and salvation?

JUDAS IS A BELIEVER JUST LIKE ANY OTHER

Jesus declared at the Last Supper that one of his own would betray him.

Judas asked:

– Is it me, Ravi? (he was already thinking about it and was looking for Jesus' confirmation).

Jesus declared:

– You said.

Judas considered it an approval. He betrayed Jesus and Jesus ended up on the cross. When Judas saw this, he threw down the money and hanged himself.

Why am I saying this?

The characterization of Judas as a traitor is not very obvious, because many apostles also denied Jesus in order to save their lives. Judas was the only one who took his own life because of Jesus' suffering.

The very final act of Judas proves that he did not betray Jesus for money but because of the belief that Jesus would show the power that Judas witnessed. This is why I consider Judas to be a great believer because he had great faith in Jesus and wanted Jesus to become king.

His mistake, like the mistake of many religious devotees, was that he believed more in the power of Jesus than in the love and humility of Jesus.

What do you think about that?

CHRISTIAN DISAGREEMENTS (or, social and religious issues)

Recently, I was a member of a theological group where I had a great response from readers on my posts. Lots of likes and lots of surprising for my standard of good comments. However, one of the admins of the group kicked me out because he didn't like my texts. I've seen this bigotry for different interpretations of the scriptures than the patterned one, so I can see why religions are considered dogma. However, I must mention that well–processed lessons are knowledge, and I have no objection to that.

Since this topic is huge, I will make a list here so that whoever wants to think about it, and I hope that we will cover certain topics in the future, because Christianity as one of the most represented religions must be purified with real spiritual interpretations, especially because of the huge number of followers. The whole society is targeted. Abolition of Christianity is not an option nor is it possible.

Here are some hints:

1. Bad interpretation of eternal hell. There is no eternal hell. There are only desires and attachments to the body and the worst, the

consequences of evil deeds. It is not true that after death you are sent to eternal hell. Jesus' statement is a hypothetic metaphor, not a law.

2. The idea of one earthly life is not correct. The soul is born as many times as it needs for the goal. There is only one true life given by God, it consists of the creation of the soul and the death of the ego and return to God.

3. Sins are not necessarily erased by repentance, prayer or donation to the church.

4. Denial of karma and reincarnation, which automatically characterizes God as unjust and merciless.

5. Jesus is not the only savior or messiah, and Christianity is not the only correct religion.

6. Faith in Jesus does not mean immediately sitting with him in heaven. One must reach the level of Jesus consciousness.

7. Polytheism is not accepted as monotheism, which is automatically an absolute omission of the knowledge offered by Christianity, thus a delusion.

8. Conviction of suicide.

These very statements create a gap towards those who might follow Christianity and worse, it provides a dead end for believers.

I highlighted what I marked as important. It would be good if everyone who wants to find their own opinion.

Don't miss out!

Visit the website below and you can sign up to receive emails whenever Vladimir Živković publishes a new book. There's no charge and no obligation.

https://books2read.com/r/B-A-HBDH-CTCBF

BOOKS 2 READ

Connecting independent readers to independent writers.

Also by Vladimir Živković

Modern Relationships
Return to God: Men and Women
Sexuality and Seduction
Return to God: Love Relationships

Savremena duhovnost
Povratak Bogu (savremena duhovnost i ljubavni odnosi)
Lagana duhovnost: dodatak knjizi "Povratak Bogu"
Razotkrivanje nasilja
Igre moći
Seksualnost i zavođenje
Bez ulepšavanja (kritika neljudskosti)
Iz kog si filma?
Lažna slika besmisla
Kakav ti je život?
Putovanje klonova
Vodič kroz psihu ateizma, religije i filozofije i njihovo dejstvo na savremenu duhovnost
Parodija ateizma
Ljubav i seks

Standalone
Destroy Evil
Love and Sex
Modern Relationships
The Book About Divine Self
Self- Help: The Understanding of Life
Duhovnost u doba korone
Spirituality in the Age of Corona
How Is Your Life?
Journey of the Clones
Duhovnost, ljubavni odnosi, seksualnost i moralna ispravnost
A Parody of Atheism
Spirituality, Love Relationships, Sexuality and Moral Correctness
A Guide to the Psyche of Atheism, Religion and Philosophy and Their Impact on Contemporary Spirituality
Znanje kao panaceja
Zabavna duhovnost
Knowledge as a Panacea
Fun Spirituality

Milton Keynes UK
Ingram Content Group UK Ltd.
UKHW041454121024
449426UK00001B/96